Praise for *Beyond Invert*

Now we can ask why! *Beyond Invert & Multiply* is a cent
and professional development. It is the perfect blend (
meaningful video clips. It is hard to imagine a classroon. ...... won't benefit from
such an exceptional resource.

—John SanGiovanni, elementary mathematics instructional facilitator
Howard County Public School System, Howard County, Maryland

Many teachers are wondering, even after studying the Common Core State Standards for Mathematics carefully, "How am I supposed to teach something I don't yet fully understand?" McNamara has anticipated our situation and designed *Beyond Invert & Multiply* to lead us, step-by-important-step, into greater understanding of the standards and ways we might teach them effectively. I want every teacher and coach to have a copy of this resource and to wear it out: mark it, bend its spine, and mine it for all its riches and classroom videos.

—Lori MacDonald, coach, K–5 mathematics
Berkeley Unified School District, Berkeley, California

Operations with fractions—a thorny topic in elementary mathematics to teach and to learn—is thoroughly demystified in *Beyond Invert & Multiply*. I've used the videos in professional development sessions; they are indispensable to show how you can present a problem to students and have them respond, knowing that misconceptions will arise.

—Josh Rosen, math specialist
Dobbs Ferry, New York

The bite-sized chapters in *Beyond Invert & Multiply* provide just the right amount of detail to allow busy practitioners access to big ideas. The activities are engaging and include clips of real classrooms using the tasks so that readers can see them in action!

—Nicole Garcia, Mathematics Research and
Design Specialist, TeachingWorks, University of Michigan

Beyond Invert & Multiply is a playbook for exemplary mathematics instruction! McNamara addresses the gap between teacher content knowledge and pedagogy while supporting educators endeavoring to meet the academic rigor of the Common Core State Standards. Emphasis on developing students' understanding of fractions is the game-changing approach essential for future success in mathematics.

—Noncy Fields, fourth-grade teacher
Ypsilanti Community Schools, Ypsilanti, Michigan

Using a combination of articulate descriptions, classroom discussion transcripts, diagrams, and videos, *Beyond Invert & Multiply* delivers clear guidance on difficult mathematics topics. Whatever your learning style, this resource will hit home.

—Arjan Khalsa, CEO
Conceptua Math

Another gem from the author of *Beyond Pizzas & Pies*! *Beyond Invert & Multiply* emphasizes the importance of *constructive struggling*—the "golden zone" for teachers and their students. The resource offers a refreshingly concise, straightforward, and accessible approach to building the foundation that all children need in order to be successful with deeper applications of mathematics in middle school and beyond.

—Ginny Gillespie, fourth-grade teacher
Malcolm X Elementary, Berkeley, California

Beyond Invert & Multiply is a "can't teach without" resource for fraction instruction. The classroom videos, text, and ready-to-use instructional activities clearly illustrate and explain how foundations of fraction sense and fraction computation are developed and supported through "best practice."

—Angela Waltrup, elementary mathematics teacher specialist
Frederick County Public Schools, Frederick County, Maryland

Beyond Invert & Multiply is exactly what educators need for guidance in implementing the Common Core Standards. The resource helps us clearly focus on making meaning, applying learning to real-life applications, and supporting students in really articulating their thinking—whether it be in small groups, in writing, or to the whole class. Consider *Beyond Invert and Multiply* your road map for daily best teaching practices.

—Jonathan Mayer, Principal
Claremont Middle School, Oakland, California

Beyond Invert & Multiply offers a perfect balance of relevant background information, research, and activities to help teachers create the opportunities our young mathematicians require in order to develop an understanding of fractions as numbers. The layout of the text along with the succinct videos make this resource well-suited for coming together to learn with colleagues.

—Justin Gregory Johns, K–5 mathematics instructional coach
American Embassy School, New Delhi, India

One reason for the persistent performance gap in mathematics is an over-emphasis on teaching for *procedural* fluency when it comes to fractions. *Beyond Invert & Multiply* offers teachers of all students specific research-based strategies for teaching what rational numbers are and how to perform operations using rational numbers in ways that develop *conceptual* understanding. This understanding will serve students well as they progress through the K–12 mathematics pipeline.

—Kyndall Brown, Executive Director
California Mathematics Project

McNamara not only has a command of mathematics content, pedagogy, and children's thinking; she masterfully weaves these areas together in this rich and accessible resource. *Beyond Invert & Multiply* will serve as a powerful resource for in-service and pre-service teachers both in developing their own content knowledge and also in supporting their students' deep conceptual understandings of fractions.

—Darrell Earnest, Assistant Professor
University of Massachusetts, Amherst

Looking for a resource to help as you implement the Number and Operations—Fractions content domain of the Common Core State Standards for Mathematics? Here it is . . . *Beyond Invert & Multiply* not only helps teachers identify what's important about operations involving fractions, but also provides contexts, classroom video clips, and activities—all backed up by research.

—Francis (Skip) Fennell, L. Stanley Bowlsbey Professor of Education and
Graduate and Professional Studies, McDaniel College, Westminster, Maryland

Beyond Invert & Multiply has made it possible for me to teach operations with fractions without "tricks." Instead, my students have a conceptual understanding of huge ideas like why dividing fractions actually results in *larger* numbers. The activities are perfect for all my students: ELLs, gifted, RSP, and general education. Thank you, Julie, for writing this!

—Morri Spang, fifth-grade teacher
San Pedro St. Elementary School, Los Angeles, California

Beyond Invert
& Multiply

Making Sense of Fraction Computation

Julie McNamara

Foreword by Deborah Loewenberg Ball

With Video Streaming

HEINEMANN
Portsmouth, NH

Heinemann
145 Maplewood Avenue, Suite 300
Portsmouth, NH 03801
www.heinemann.com

Cataloging-in-Publication data is on file with the Library of Congress.

ISBN-13: 978-0-325-13758-2
EISBN-13: 978-0-325-13938-8

Editor: Jamie Ann Cross
Production: Denise A. Botelho
Cover design: Jan Streitburger, Crescent Hill Studio
Interior design: Lisa Delgado, Delgado and Company
Composition: Publishers' Design and Production Services, Inc.
Cover images: © Anteromite/Shutterstock.com
Interior images: Friday's Films
Manufacturing: Gerard Clancy

Printed in the United States of America on acid-free paper.
1 2 3 4 5   GP   26 25 24 23 22   PO34415

A Message from Heinemann

Heinemann's math professional resources are written by educators, for educators, to support student-centered teaching and learning. Our authors provide classroom-tested guidance, advice, and proven best practices to help teachers increase their comfort and confidence with teaching math. We believe a focus on reasoning and understanding is the pathway to helping students make sense of the mathematics they're learning.

This resource was originally published by Math Solutions, a company long dedicated to similar ideals and aims as Heinemann. In 2022, Math Solutions Publications became part of Heinemann. While the logo on the cover is different, the heart of Math Solutions lives in these pages: that teaching math well calls for increasing our understanding of the math we teach, seeking deeper insights into how students learn mathematics, and refining our lessons to best promote students' learning.

To learn more about our resources and authors, please visit Heinemann.com/Math.

*To the dedicated teachers who believe that all students
are capable of making sense of mathematics*

Brief Contents

Activities

Reproducibles

Activity-Specific Reproducibles

Reproducibles Used with More Than One Activity

All reproducibles are available as downloadable, printable versions at http://hein.pub/MathOLR. Registration information and key code can be found on page xxviii in the frontmatter.

Teaching mathematics is so much harder than knowing or doing math oneself. Knowing math is necessary but not at all sufficient for helping others understand it. Of course one certainly can't teach something that one doesn't know. But the work involved in making explicit what particular concepts or operations mean, and why certain procedures work, is different from solving one's own problems or justifying one's own solutions. Teaching requires more than this sort of explicit, unpacked, sense-making approach to understanding. Helping others learn demands a flexibility with ways of explaining and representing the content—when one approach doesn't seem to help, teachers need alternatives.

But teaching is also more than explaining content *to* learners. Teaching involves listening to learners talk, reading learners' mathematical writing, and trying to make sense of what learners know—and also what they don't. The mathematical agility required in making sense of someone else's mathematical thinking or work is demanding. And teachers must do this with twenty-five, thirty, or even more students at the same time. This sort of mathematical work depends on what my colleagues and I have called *specialized* mathematical knowledge, because it is so particular to the specific uses to which teachers have to put their mathematical understanding.

A big challenge for most of us who teach elementary students is that when we were their age, we were not taught in ways that unpacked the mathematical meanings or exposed the underlying ideas. Often there was more focus on memorizing rules and developing fluency. If this was what we experienced when we learned math, it means that developing our skills as teachers often involves unlearning how we learned math *and* learning it in new ways.

Beyond Invert & Multiply is a mathematics resource written expressly for the work of teaching. The sequel to *Beyond Pizzas & Pies, Second Edition* (McNamara and Shaughnessy, 2015), *Beyond Invert & Multiply* delves into the mathematics of fraction computation, an area of elementary mathematics that is often opaque to students, and over which they often stumble. For many children, fraction computation is where they begin to struggle with math. This not only affects their learning but also their confidence and interest. And facility with fractions is one of the most important foundations for middle school and beyond. Further, when students struggle, they sometimes begin to see mathematics as senseless and not learnable. The content can seem so strange compared to their earlier work with whole numbers. Now $\frac{3}{8}$ is less than $\frac{1}{2}$, even though 3 is greater than 1 and 8 is greater than 2. And adding $\frac{3}{8} + \frac{1}{2}$ is not $\frac{4}{10}$. Multiplying fractions seems easier—after all, $\frac{3}{8} \times \frac{1}{2}$ *is* equal to the products of the numerator and denominator, or $\frac{3}{16}$. But why the product, $\frac{3}{16}$, is less than either $\frac{3}{8}$ or $\frac{1}{2}$ is not obvious. Doesn't multiplying two numbers result in a "bigger" number? And dividing fractions is perhaps the most mystifying of all. How can $1\frac{3}{4} \div \frac{1}{2} = 3\frac{1}{2}$? But the procedure—invert and multiply—yields just that. The problem is that, while students become more and more mystified, and less and less connected to the meaning of what they are doing, we as teachers are often unprepared to help. When many of us were in fourth grade, the procedures were enough and no one regularly asked what the answers meant. Even if we ourselves had experience making sense of fractions in school, we still often have more to learn in order to be able to help learners—who are not us—understand the content.

Beyond Invert & Multiply is a professional mathematics resource for teachers. It opens the mathematics up with diagrams, clear explanations, and classroom scenarios. Ideas and procedures that seemed opaque are made transparent and reasonable. Math that was not part of our own education suddenly makes sense. The insights that Julie McNamara's expositions offer are illuminating and exciting. But *Beyond Invert & Multiply* is more than that. It is a resource for our work, the work of teaching. Filled with examples from classroom teaching of fraction concepts and computation, the resource gives activities, tasks, and tours of what our learning can be like. Readers who study this resource and watch the video clips will learn math from the teaching described and shown. They will also learn ideas about teaching.

As the standards are raised for students, the challenges for teachers are also higher. This resource could not be more timely, more respectful of, and responsive to teaching. It offers just the right amount of support to help teachers provide skillful mathematics instruction for all their students—and it's concrete and flexibly usable. Confronted with teaching the subtraction of fractions, a teacher could delve directly into Chapter 4 without reading the previous chapters and immediately be immersed in the ideas relevant to the mathematical and instructional demands of this topic. Written for the practice of *teaching* mathematics, *Beyond Invert & Multiply* is a mathematics resource essential for the work of teachers.

By supporting teachers, *Beyond Invert & Multiply* will help young learners arrive at middle school equipped with foundations of understanding and confidence. And their learning, in the end, is the point.

—Deborah Loewenberg Ball, William H. Payne Collegiate Professor, School of Education, University of Michigan

VIDEO CLIP

Introduction

Watch the video clip "Introduction." Talk with a friend or colleague; what do you see in the introduction that makes you most excited about *Beyond Invert & Multiply*?

To view this video clip, scan the QR code or access via http://hein.pub/MathOLR

Why This Resource?

Over the past several years fractions, as a topic in school mathematics, have received a great deal of attention. This is due, in large part, to growing research evidence that the majority of students enter middle school with limited understanding of fractions and, as a result, struggle with much of the mathematics content of middle school and beyond. With the Common Core State Standards for Mathematics, as well as other standards documents, the importance of understanding fractions as numbers has become a foundational aspect of fraction instruction in grades 3 and above. In addition, as students begin computing with fractions in subsequent grades, understanding fractions as numbers is central to helping students calculate with accuracy, efficiency, and understanding.

Why Is Fraction Computation So Hard?

Children have an intuitive sense about halving (as well as a very well-developed sense of fairness!) so their first encounter with fractions likely happens before they enter school. They may have shared a sandwich with a sibling or split a bag of candies with a friend. In these cases, children are concerned with making sure all parties get the same amount (or fair share), but once the partitioning is completed, it is unlikely that the term *half* is anything other than a label for the smaller portions, not a mathematical concept. The term *the larger half*, as in "She got the larger half!" is evidence of this phenomenon.

In the primary grades, students begin partitioning areas into fractional parts with consideration given to the parts being equal. Fraction names such as *halves*, *fourths*, and *eighths* are introduced, but are not yet labeled using numerical notation. Children as young as first grade can solve simple problems involving fraction computation when the problems are presented in a meaningful context involving sharing (Carpenter 2014). They may draw the partitions to indicate each share, but typically do not know how to label the parts using fraction notation.

When students encounter formal fraction notation (usually in grade 3), they now must understand that fraction names such as *one-fourth* are not just a label for a part or portion, but describe a relationship between the part and the whole. In the fraction $\frac{1}{4}$, for example, students must understand that the digits 1 and 4 represent a relationship and must be considered differently than in the number 14. Depending on the context, $\frac{1}{4}$ may mean $\frac{1}{4}$ of one item or unit, $\frac{1}{4}$ of a group of items, or $\frac{1}{4}$ of a distance or interval (McNamara and Shaughnessy 2015). When students begin working on fraction computation, they must be able to abstract from the specifics of the context and operate on the fractions as numbers. For example, the computation involved in the following two problems is the same even though the answers represent very different lengths of time:

1. Shweta worked on her homework for $\frac{1}{4}$ of an hour before dinner and $\frac{1}{4}$ of an hour after dinner. What fraction of an hour did Shweta spend on her homework?

2. Lila spent 24 hours working on her science project. She spent $\frac{1}{4}$ of that time collecting data on Monday and $\frac{1}{4}$ of her time collecting data on Wednesday. She spent the rest of the time analyzing and writing up her results. What fraction of her time did Lila spend on data collection?

Both problems involve adding $\frac{1}{4}$ and $\frac{1}{4}$, however in Problem 1, the actual time Shweta spent on her homework is less than one hour and in Problem 2, the actual time Lila spent on her project is 12 hours. Being able to move flexibly between realistic contexts as shown here and decontextualized computation such as adding $\frac{1}{4} + \frac{1}{4}$ is an essential aspect of understanding fraction computation. Unless students are provided ample opportunity to develop an understanding of fractions as numbers, their success with problems such as these is unlikely.

Another challenge students have with fraction computation results from their previous experience with whole numbers. Students may be presented with three whole numbers such as 6, 4, and 24, as a *fact family*, and are often told that the largest number (in this case, 24) is the product in the multiplication problems *4 × 6 = 24* and *6 × 4 = 24* and the dividend in the division problems *24 ÷ 6 = 4* and *24 ÷ 4 = 6*. It is not unusual for students to generalize this to mean that multiplication makes things bigger and division makes things smaller. This generalization (which makes good sense when working with whole numbers) can cause a lot of confusion when students encounter multiplication and division problems involving fractions. If students don't understand that $\frac{1}{2}$ is a number halfway between 0 and 1, they have little chance of understanding why multiplying 24 by $\frac{1}{2}$ results in a product less than 24 and dividing 24 by $\frac{1}{2}$ results in a quotient that is greater than 24.

In addition, it is not uncommon for students to learn rules and procedures for operating on fractions with little understanding, resulting in confusion over which procedure to apply when. For example, students may have been successful multiplying across numerators and denominators and then (unsuccessfully) try the same approach with addition. Or students taught to "invert and multiply" or "keep, change, flip" to solve division problems with fractions may become confused about which part of the problem to invert, keep, change, or flip.

This resource and the accompanying video clips are designed to support you as you help your students develop a robust understanding of fractions and as they learn to calculate with accuracy, efficiency, and understanding. *Beyond Invert & Multiply* builds on the foundational understandings that are described in *Beyond Pizzas & Pies: 10 Essential Strategies for Developing Fraction Sense, Second Edition* (McNamara and Shaughnessy 2015) and applies them to situations involving computation. As in *Beyond Pizzas & Pies*, the approach is designed to build on students' fraction sense because, "Fraction sense is tied to common sense: Students with fraction sense can reason about fractions and don't apply rules and procedures blindly; nor do they give nonsensical answers to problems involving fractions" (McNamara and Shaughnessy 2015).

How This Resource Is Organized

Beyond Invert & Multiply is not necessarily intended to be read from cover to cover. Each section addresses different aspects of fraction computation. Different sections may have different levels of significance for you depending on your grade level and your students' particular needs. The order in which you read the sections doesn't matter; each section is written to stand alone.

This resource is organized into four parts:

- Part I addresses the meaning of fractions and understanding fractions as numbers. Chapter 1, Making Sense: Fractions as Numbers, contains the following:

  - *CCSS Connections:* The chapter begins with a connection to the relevant Common Core State Standards.

  - *Classroom Scenario:* The chapter addresses a common challenge that students encounter as they learn to operate with fractions. Some of these challenges may be tied to fraction notation, some may be connected to students' previous experience with whole numbers and fractions, and some may be the result of misapplying rules and procedures students learned when working with fractions. Each scenario is presented in the context of a fictional classroom episode in the third-grade classroom of Ms. Taylor, the fourth-grade classroom of Mrs. Ahmed, the fifth-grade classrooms of Ms. Chu and Mr. Gregory, and the sixth-grade classroom of Mr. Frank. While the exact episodes and students are fictional, the students' comments and struggles are taken from my work in classrooms as either teacher or researcher. The challenges are also not grade-level specific; you may find your sixth graders struggle in the same way as Ms. Taylor's third graders or your fourth graders may have some of the same difficulties as Ms. Chu's fifth graders.

- *What's the Math?* This section is intended to clarify the mathematics that is being addressed in the section.
- *What's the Research?* As teachers are asked to do more and more during the school day, it is imperative that we no longer continue with practices because "that's the way we've always done things." The research helps us to identify strategies, contexts, and representations that will ensure we get the most out of our instructional time, as well as those that may be problematic and/or limited.
- *Classroom Activities:* The chapter includes activities designed to help your students learn to calculate with accuracy, efficiency, and understanding. Materials lists, reproducibles, and examples of student projects are included. In addition, the accompanying video clips feature actual classroom footage of students and teachers engaged in several of the *Classroom Activities*. These activities are not meant to replace your current curriculum, but you may find that they will allow you to provide experiences for your students that help them further develop their ability to make sense of fraction computation.
- *Video Clips:* Chapters 1, 3, 6, 7, and 8 include video clips that were filmed in actual classrooms; see the tables on pages xxix–xxxii for a listing of clips by grade and chapter.
- *Wrapping It Up:* Each section ends with closing comments, study questions, and suggestions for additional resources when appropriate.
- Part II begins with Chapter 2, Developing Awareness: Addition and Subtraction Problem Types. This chapter is followed by two *Making Sense* chapters that address fraction addition as well as addressing fraction subtraction. The *Making Sense* chapters follow the same format as in Chapter 1.
- Part III begins with Chapter 5, Developing Awareness: Multiplication and Division Problem Types. The *Making Sense* Chapters 6 and 7 follow and address fraction multiplication as well as fraction division. These chapters follow the same format as in Chapter 1.
- Part IV begins with Chapter 8, Developing Awareness: Six Strategies for Fostering Student Talk About Fractions and addresses the challenging topic of mathematical discourse.

Get Started!

The importance of helping students make sense of fractions and fraction computation cannot be overstated. The scenarios and research findings presented in the following pages illustrate many of the challenges students without fraction sense face as they attempt to solve problems involving fraction computation. By providing opportunities for your students to investigate, discuss, revise, expand, and refine their understanding of fractions and fraction computation, you can prepare them for success with deeper application tasks they will encounter in middle school and beyond. In addition, this preparation will help them better understand, appreciate, and navigate the increasingly complex role that mathematics plays in the modern world.

A Letter from Math Coach Lori MacDonald

I cannot recall a time in my professional life when I've been more grateful for a resource. Teachers in Berkeley have been working hard learning the Common Core standards, paying special attention to the new emphasis on fractions. The standards seem logical, but we have many questions and some concerns as we enter our second year teaching them. Julie McNamara, in an immeasurably helpful way, has anticipated our situation and designed *Beyond Invert & Multiply: Making Sense of Fraction Computation* to lead us, step-by-important-step, into greater understanding of the standards and ways we might teach them effectively.

Many teachers are wondering, even after studying the standards carefully, "How am I supposed to teach something I don't yet fully understand?" My answer is, read *Beyond Invert & Multiply*. Here's a quick look at how each section provides invaluable support.

Classroom Scenario

In the "Classroom Scenario" sections of *Beyond Invert & Multiply*, Julie gets right inside our heads. Through her deft analysis of teachers' thinking process, Julie assures the reader that she understands our need to be led through a guided process to gain greater understanding. If we could have mastered the standards in one reading, we would have. Julie begins each chapter with us in the classroom as we struggle with knowing how best to teach these unfamiliar concepts.

What's the Math?

Julie then begins a short but effective section of direction instruction, "What's the Math?," and we are listening, because we know Julie gets it.

What's the Research?

Having then acquired a better understanding of the concept at hand, we are pushed to consider what the research says. *Where are the typical misunderstandings among students? Among teachers? What has been shown to be most effective in terms of framing the concept?*

Classroom Activities

Then, once our trust has been earned and our understanding increased, right about the time we're thinking, "This is great, but I don't have time to translate this into lessons," *Beyond Invert & Multiply* gives us "Classroom Activities," replete with reproducibles and video clips demonstrating how to teach the concept.

Wrapping It Up

In "Wrapping It Up," we are asked questions that show us how far we've come and challenge us to set concrete goals for implementing what we've learned.

Throughout the book, the reader feels as if she has a personal math guide. This is not an academic book, simply offering some good ideas on how you might approach teaching fractions. It is a systematic walk through of the Common Core State Standards for Mathematics. In the middle of explaining a new approach taken in the CCSSM, Julie reminds us of how previous standards addressed similar concepts. By reminding us of how we previously understood (and probably taught) various concepts, our learning of the new standards is greatly facilitated. No ideas in this book are offered in a vacuum; Julie creates a context for all she discusses.

What a gift *Beyond Invert & Multiply* is to teachers. Personal. Practical. Professional. I want every teacher and coach in Berkeley Unified to have a copy of this resource and to wear it out: mark it, bend its spine, and mine it for all its riches and classroom videos.

—Lori MacDonald, coach, K–5 mathematics
Berkeley Unified School District, California

Summary of Connections with the Common Core State Standards

The following connections are also featured at the beginning of each of the corresponding chapters; they are included here as well for quick reference.

Chapter	CCSS Content Standards: Number and Operations: Fractions (NF); Geometry (G)
1 Making Sense: Fractions as Numbers	**Prerequisite Standards** **2.G.A.3:** Partition circles and rectangles into two, three, or four equal shares, describe the shares using the words halves, thirds, half of, a third of, etc., and describe the whole as two halves, three thirds, four fourths. Recognize that equal shares of identical wholes need not have the same shape. **Standards Addressed** **3.NF.A.1:** Understand a fraction $\frac{1}{b}$ as the quantity formed by 1 part when a whole is partitioned into b equal parts; understand a fraction $\frac{a}{b}$ as the quantity formed by [a] parts of size $\frac{1}{b}$. **3.NF.A.2:** Understand a fraction as a number on the number line; represent fractions on a number line diagram. **3.NF.A.3:** Explain equivalence of fractions in special cases, and compare fractions by reasoning about their size. **4.NF.B.3:** Understand a fraction $\frac{a}{b}$ with $a > 1$ as a sum of fractions $\frac{1}{b}$.
3 Making Sense: Addition with Fractions	**Prerequisite Standards** **3.NF.A.1:** Understand a fraction $\frac{1}{b}$ as the quantity formed by 1 part when a whole is partitioned into b equal parts; understand a fraction $\frac{a}{b}$ as the quantity formed by [a] parts of size $\frac{1}{b}$. **3.NF.A.2:** Understand a fraction as a number on the number line; represent fractions on a number line diagram. **Standards Addressed** **4.NF.B.3:** Understand a fraction $\frac{a}{b}$ with $a > 1$ as a sum of fractions $\frac{1}{b}$. **4.NF.B.3a:** Understand addition and subtraction of fractions as joining and separating parts referring to the same whole. **4.NF.B.3b:** Decompose a fraction into a sum of fractions with the same denominator in more than one way, recording each decomposition by an equation. Justify decompositions, e.g., by using a visual fraction model. **4.NF.B.3c:** Add and subtract mixed numbers with like denominators, e.g., by replacing each mixed number with an equivalent fraction, and/or by using properties of operations and the relationship between addition and subtraction. **5.NF.A.1:** Add and subtract fractions with unlike denominators (including mixed numbers) by replacing given fractions with equivalent fractions in such a way as to produce an equivalent sum or difference of fractions with like denominators.

(continued)

Chapter	CCSS Content Standards: Number and Operations: Fractions (NF); Geometry (G)
4 Making Sense: Subtraction with Fractions	**Prerequisite Standards** **3.NF.A.1:** Understand a fraction $\frac{1}{b}$ as the quantity formed by 1 part when a whole is partitioned into b equal parts; understand a fraction $\frac{a}{b}$ as the quantity formed by a parts of size $\frac{1}{b}$. **3.NF.A.2:** Understand a fraction as a number on the number line; represent fractions on a number line diagram. **Standards Addressed** **4.NF.B.3:** Understand a fraction $\frac{a}{b}$ with $a > 1$ as a sum of fractions $\frac{1}{b}$. **4.NF.B.3a:** Understand addition and subtraction of fractions as joining and separating parts referring to the same whole. **4.NF.B.3b:** Decompose a fraction into a sum of fractions with the same denominator in more than one way, recording each decomposition by an equation. Justify decompositions, e.g., by using a visual fraction model. **4.NF.B.3c:** Add and subtract mixed numbers with like denominators, e.g., by replacing each mixed number with an equivalent fraction, and/or by using properties of operations and the relationship between addition and subtraction. **5.NF.A.1:** Add and subtract fractions with unlike denominators (including mixed numbers) by replacing given fractions with equivalent fractions in such a way as to produce an equivalent sum or difference of fractions with like denominators.
6 Making Sense: Multiplication with Fractions	**Prerequisite Standards** **3.NF.A.1:** Understand a fraction $\frac{1}{b}$ as the quantity formed by 1 part when a whole is partitioned into b equal parts; understand a fraction $\frac{a}{b}$ as the quantity formed by a parts of size $\frac{1}{b}$. **Standards Addressed** **4.NF.B.3:** Understand a fraction $\frac{a}{b}$ with $a > 1$ as a sum of fractions $\frac{1}{b}$. **4.NF.B.4:** Apply and extend previous understandings of multiplication to multiply a fraction by a whole number. **5.NF.B.4:** Apply and extend previous understandings of multiplication to multiply a fraction or whole number by a fraction. **5.NF.B.6:** Solve real-world problems involving multiplication of fractions and mixed numbers.

Chapter	CCSS Content Standards: Number and Operations: Fractions (NF); Geometry (G)
7 Making Sense: **Division with Fractions**	**Prerequisite Standards** **3.NF.A.1:** Understand a fraction $\frac{1}{b}$ as the quantity formed by 1 part when a whole is partitioned into b equal parts; understand a fraction $\frac{a}{b}$ as the quantity formed by a parts of size $\frac{1}{b}$. **3.NF.A.2:** Understand a fraction as a number on the number line; represent fractions on a number line diagram. **4.NF.B.3:** Understand a fraction $\frac{a}{b}$ with $a > 1$ as a sum of fractions $\frac{1}{b}$. **5.NF.B.3:** Interpret a fraction as division of the numerator by the denominator ($\frac{a}{b} = a \div b$). Solve word problems involving division of whole numbers leading to answers in the form of fractions or mixed numbers, e.g., by using visual fraction models or equations to represent the problem. **Standards Addressed** **5.NF.B.7:** Apply and extend previous understanding of division to divide unit fractions by whole numbers and whole numbers by unit fractions. **6.NS.A.1:** Interpret and compute quotients of fractions, and solve word problems involving division of fractions by fractions, e.g., by using visual fraction models and equations to represent the problem.

How to Access Online Resources

Readers have several options for accessing the video clips. Either scan the QR code (with a QR code reader app of your choice) that appears within the video clip section in the text or enter the corresponding URLs in your browser. If you would like to access all the clips at once or download the reproducibles, follow these instructions:

1. Go to http://hein.pub/MathOLR and click or tap the Create New Account button at the bottom of the Log In form.
2. Create an account. You will receive a confirmation email when your account has been created.
3. Once your account has been created, you will be taken to the Product Registration page. Click Register on the product you would like to access (in this case, *Beyond Invert & Multiply*).

KEY CODE
BIM 4. Enter **key code BIM** and click or tap the Submit Key Code button.
5. Click or tap the Complete Registration button.
6. To access videos, video viewing guidelines, and online resources at any time or register another product, visit your account page.

Guidelines for Watching Videos of Teaching

The teachers who agreed to be recorded in these videos have complex and challenging classrooms, just like you. When we watch videos of others it is easy to see things that we might do differently. It is then all to easy to move to a critical stance, focusing on what the teacher "should" have done differently. But we have found that such a stance is not helpful for learning.

These videos are not scripted or rehearsed. They are real classroom sessions. Remember that teaching is a complicated activity, in which the teacher is required to do many things at once. As you watch these videos, alone or with others, we recommend following these rules:

1. Assume that there are many things you don't know about the students, the classroom, and the shared history of the teacher and students in the video.
2. Assume good intent and expertise on the part of the teacher. If you cannot understand his or her actions, try to hypothesize what might have motivated him or her.
3. Keep focused on your observations about what students are getting out of the talk and interaction.
4. Keep focused on how the classroom discourse is serving the mathematical goals of the lesson. (Chapin, O'Connor, and Anderson 2013, xxi)

Video Clips by Chapter

Page Number	Video Clip	Length	Title	Grade/Teacher
Chapter 1				
16	1a	6:22	Placing $\frac{1}{2}$ on the Number Line	Grade 5/Ms. Kretschmar
17	1b	1:28	Using Cuisenaire Rods to Place $\frac{1}{3}$ on the Number Line	Grade 5/Ms. Kretschmar
18	1c	:53	Using Cuisenaire Rods to Place $\frac{3}{2}$ on the Number Line	Grade 5/Ms. Kretschmar
19	1d	1:19	Deciding Where to Place $\frac{11}{3}$ on the Number Line	Grade 5/Ms. Kretschmar
Chapter 3				
51	3a	1:38	Reviewing the "Make a 10" Strategy	Grade 5/Ms. Kretschmar
52	3b	:51	Introducing "Get to the Whole"	Grade 5/Ms. Kretschmar
53	3c	2:23	$\frac{3}{4} + \frac{3}{4}$: Will's Strategy	Grade 5/Ms. Kretschmar
53	3d	1:20	$\frac{3}{4} + \frac{3}{4}$: Belen's Strategy	Grade 5/Ms. Kretschmar
54	3e	1:16	$\frac{3}{5} + \frac{4}{5}$: Malaya's Strategy	Grade 5/Ms. Kretschmar
54	3f	:39	$\frac{3}{5} + \frac{4}{5}$: Yuli's Use of Academic Language	Grade 5/Ms. Kretschmar
Chapter 6				
96	6a	3:57	Introducing Activity 6.1: Multiplication Patterns	Grade 4/Ms. Lee
97	6b	1:05	Noticing Patterns in Factors and Products	Grade 4/Ms. Lee
97	6c	1:05	Moving from Additive to Multiplicative Language	Grade 4/Ms. Lee
98	6d	:28	What Number Is $\frac{1}{2}$ of 1?	Grade 4/Ms. Lee
99	6e	1:59	Multiplication as Repeated Addition	Grade 4/Ms. Lee
104	6f	1:35	What Do We Know About 6 x 2$\frac{1}{2}$?	Grade 4/Ms. McNamara

(continued)

Video Clips by Chapter (cont'd)

Page Number	Video Clip	Length	Title	Grade/Teacher
104	6g	1:39	"6 x $2\frac{1}{2}$ Has to Be Greater Than $2\frac{1}{2}$"	Grade 4/Ms. McNamara
105	6h	1:15	Applying the Distributive Property to Reason About the Product of 6 x $2\frac{1}{2}$	Grade 4/Ms. McNamara
105	6i	3:12	$4\frac{1}{2}$ Is More Than 4 But Less Than 5	Grade 4/Ms. McNamara
Chapter 7				
128	7a	2:25	Introducing Activity 7.2: How Long? How Far?	Grade 6/Mr. Trenado and Ms. McNamara
128	7b	1:32	Comparing the Two Jogging Experiences	Grade 6/Mr. Trenado
130	7c	2:36	How Many $\frac{1}{4}$s Are in 1?	Grade 6/Mr. Trenado
131	7d	2:46	How Many $\frac{1}{4}$s Are in 2?	Grade 6/Mr. Trenado
131	7e	1:37	How Many $\frac{1}{3}$s Are in 2?	Grade 6/Mr. Trenado
Chapter 8				
143	8a	1:02	Multiplication Patterns	Grade 4/Ms. Lee
144	8b	2:40	Muhammad's Strategy for Adding $\frac{5}{9}$ and $\frac{8}{9}$	Grade 5/Ms. Kretschmar
145	8c	1:42	Using the Cuisenaire Rods to Explain Equivalent Fractions	Grade 6/Mr. Trenado
146	8d	4:57	What Do You Notice About the Numerators and Denominators of Fractions Equal to $\frac{1}{2}$?	Grade 5/Ms. Kretschmar and Ms. McNamara
147	8e	2:09	Ms. Lee Revoices Ashley's Justification	Grade 4/Ms. Lee
148	8f	2:36	Julian Restates Carlos's Answer	Grade 6/Mr. Trenado
149	8g	6:23	Multiple Students Share Their Reasoning About Placing $\frac{1}{2}$ on the Number Line	Grade 5/Ms. Kretschmar
150	8h	1:17	"Tell Us More About That"	Grade 4/Ms. McNamara
151	8i	:47	Posing a "Thinking Question"	Grade 4/Ms. McNamara

Video Clips by Grade, Including Demographics

Demographics: *The student body at Lighthouse Community Charter School comprises 81 percent Hispanic, 9 percent African American, 5 percent Multiethnic, 3 percent Asian/Pacific Islander, 1 percent Middle Eastern, and 1 percent Caucasian. Eight-one percent of students are English learners. Eight-six percent of the students receive free or reduced price lunch.*

Grade	Teacher	Video Clips
Grades 4, 5, 6	Julie McNamara is the author of *Beyond Invert and Multiply* and is thrilled to be a guest teacher. She is sure she learned far more from the students than they learned from her!	Julie appears as a guest teacher in several of the following clips.
Grade 4	Ms. Lee teaches third and fourth grade. She has been teaching for ten years, and has previously taught first and second grades as well. Ms. Lee places a high priority on student-led discussions and emphasizing multiple ways of problem solving in her teaching.	6a Introducing Activity 6.1: Multiplication Patterns 6b Noticing Patterns in Factors and Products 6c Moving from Additive to Multiplicative Language 6d What Number is $\frac{1}{2}$ of 1? 6e Multiplication as Repeated Addition 6f What Do We Know About $6 \times 2\frac{1}{2}$? 6g "$6 \times 2\frac{1}{2}$ Has to Be Greater Than $2\frac{1}{2}$" 6h Applying the Distributive Property to Reason About the Product of $6 \times 2\frac{1}{2}$ 6i $4\frac{1}{2}$ Is More Than 4 But Less Than 5 8a Multiplication Patterns 8e Ms. Lee Revoices Ashley's Justification 8h "Tell Us More About That" 8i Posing a "Thinking Question

(continued)

Grade	Teacher	Video Clips
Grade 5	Ms. Kretschmar teaches fifth- and sixth-grade math and science. She has been teaching and learning from her students for seventeen years. She puts a high priority on looking deeply at student work and listening to student thinking to inform instruction.	1a Placing $\frac{1}{2}$ on the Number Line 1b Using Cuisenaire Rods to Place $\frac{1}{3}$ on the Number Line 1c Using Cuisenaire Rods to Place $\frac{3}{2}$ on the Number Line 1d Deciding Where to Place $\frac{11}{3}$ on the Number Line 3a Reviewing the "Make a 10" Strategy 3b Introducing "Get to the Whole" 3c $\frac{3}{4} + \frac{3}{4}$: Will's Strategy 3d $\frac{3}{4} + \frac{3}{4}$: Belen's Strategy 3e $\frac{3}{5} + \frac{4}{5}$: Malaya's Strategy 3f $\frac{3}{5} + \frac{4}{5}$: Yuli's Use of Academic Language 8b Muhammad's Strategy for Adding $\frac{5}{9}$ and $\frac{8}{9}$ 8d What Do You Notice About the Numerators and Denominators of Fractions Equal to $\frac{1}{2}$? 8g Multiple Students Share Their Reasoning About Placing $\frac{1}{2}$ on the Number Line
Grade 6	Mr. Trenado taught sixth-grade math and science at Lighthouse Community Charter School. He now teaches history and English at Lazear Charter Academy in Oakland, California. He has been teaching for four years and has worked to build great relationships with students and their families. Mr. Trenado grew up in East Oakland in the community he teaches and loves to learn about best practices in teaching.	7a Introducing Activity 7.2: How Long? How Far? 7b Comparing the Two Jogging Experiences 7c How Many $\frac{1}{4}$s Are in 1? 7d How Many $\frac{1}{4}$s Are in 2? 7e How Many $\frac{1}{3}$s Are in 2? 8c Using the Cuisenaire Rods to Explain Equivalent Fractions 8f Julian Restates Carlos's Answer

What Is a Fraction?

Making Sense
Fractions as Numbers

CCSS Connections

Prerequisite Standards

2.G.A.3: Partition circles and rectangles into two, three, or four equal shares, describe the shares using the words halves, thirds, half of, a third of, etc., and describe the whole as two halves, three thirds, four fourths. Recognize that equal shares of identical wholes need not have the same shape.

Standards Addressed

3.NF.A.1: Understand a fraction 1/b as the quantity formed by 1 part when a whole is partitioned into b equal parts; understand a fraction a/b as the quantity formed by [a] parts of size 1/b.

3.NF.A.2: Understand a fraction as a number on the number line; represent fractions on a number line diagram.

3.NF.A.3: Explain equivalence of fractions in special cases, and compare fractions by reasoning about their size.

4.NF.B.3: Understand a fraction a/b with a > 1 as a sum of fractions 1/b.

As Ms. Taylor began to plan her fractions unit she was a bit baffled about how to help her third graders understand fractions as numbers. Working with fractions on number lines was new to her and she knew most of her students had little experience with number lines. She was confident that her students understood fractions as parts of areas, and could clearly articulate the importance of knowing the size of the whole and the necessity of creating equal-sized parts when partitioning areas and lengths. She was less sure, however, how to help them understand and represent fractions as numbers on the number line.

Ms. Taylor felt that before placing fractions on the number line her students would need practice placing whole numbers on the line. She decided to have her students create a "human number line" by giving them numbers and having them place themselves at the appropriate intervals. In order to make room for all of her students and to take advantage of the nice weather, Ms. Taylor chose to create the human number line on the playground. The morning before the lesson she prepared index cards with the numbers 0 to 27, with one number written on each card; she dug out some old chalk from the back of her desk, scoped out a good spot on the playground for the human number line, and on the asphalt, drew a long line with an arrow on each end.

When Ms. Taylor had all of her students gathered in front of the chalk line she asked students what they saw.

"It looks like a line. Or is it a line segment?" asked Ty, who had an older sister at the middle school.

"I think we're going to have a race!" called out Phoebe excitedly. Several other students nodded in agreement.

"I bet we're gonna do math," suggested Chandra, ever the pragmatist.

"Chandra guessed it—we are going to do some math. And Ty is also correct—I've drawn a line on the pavement and we're going to use it to make a human number line."

After briefly discussing the difference between a line and a line segment, Ms. Taylor randomly passed out the cards to the students. Once all the cards were passed out she asked who had a card that would be good to start with. Several students raised their hands; Ms. Taylor asked them to hold their cards so that everyone could see them. After looking over the numbers on the cards several students suggested that Mikhal should go first, because he had the number 0 and that was the smallest number shown.

Ms. Taylor asked Mikhal to walk to the line and decide where he should stand. He chose a spot close to one of the arrows. Several students indicated that they agreed with his placement by giving the class hand signal showing agreement.

"OK, it looks like everyone agrees with where Mikhal is standing." Looking around at the students Ms. Taylor then asked, "Who's next?"

Almost as though choreographed, the students with the cards showing numbers 1 through 8 fell in line next to Mikhal. Ms. Taylor was pleased that the students were ordering the numbers correctly, but she was concerned that they were not attending to the size of the intervals between each number. Calling a halt to any more students joining the line, Ms. Taylor asked the students who had not yet joined the line what they noticed. Several students commented that the numbers were all in the right order but no one brought up the issue of the different distances between each number. Ms. Taylor decided this was a good time to review some of the important aspects of the number line.

"I'm really glad that you noticed that the numbers are all in the correct order. That is one of the important principles about number lines. Another important thing about number lines is that the distance between neighboring whole numbers needs to be the same—this is called the *unit interval*. Take a look at our number line—are the unit intervals the same between each whole number?"

Ms. Taylor knew that not all of the third graders understood this idea but she also knew that the discussion that resulted from her question would help them grasp it.

"They look pretty good at first but then they start to squish together," Chandra suggested.

"I agree with Chandra," Ana chimed in. "Maybe we should measure to make sure all the spaces are the same."

"What do the rest of you think of Ana's idea? Would measuring help?" Ms. Taylor asked.

After some lively discussion the class decided that the unit intervals on the human number line should be measured by Ms. Taylor's stride. Starting at zero, Ms. Taylor took one long step and drew a tick mark with chalk. The student holding the card with the number 1 stood on the tick mark. As Ms. Taylor continued walking along the line and marking the intervals, students came and stood at the appropriate spot. After all of the students were on the line Ms. Taylor decided to place one more number on the line.

"I have one more number to place on the line," Ms. Taylor reached into her pocket and pulled out a blank index card. She quickly wrote the number $\frac{1}{2}$ on the card and held it up for the students to see. "Where on the line should I go?" A few students raised their hands but most looked at Ms. Taylor confusedly.

"Talk to your neighbor and discuss where on the line one-half should go," Ms. Taylor suggested, knowing that partner talk was an effective strategy for generating ideas and preparing students for discussion.

After a few minutes of partner talk, Ms. Taylor asked her question again. "Where on the line should I go?"

Several pairs of students raised their hands confidently. Calling on one of the partnerships, Ms. Taylor was quite surprised by what she heard.

"We think you should go between one and two!" Carlo, the spokesman for the pair, said. Carlo's partner smiled and several students indicated their agreement.

"Any other ideas?" Ms. Taylor asked, interested to see what other ideas were discussed during the partner talk.

"Between zero and one!"

"In the middle of one and two!"

"How 'bout on the other side of zero?"

"Maybe in the middle of all the numbers on the line?"

"I'm hearing a lot of ideas about where one-half should go. This is a good time for us to wrap up our human number line and go inside and figure out the answer to this question." Ms. Taylor led her students back into the classroom, happy that they were so engaged and challenged by her question. She drew a number line on the board and turned to her class.

"Now where were we?" she began with a smile.

Understanding fractions as numbers is essential for students to be successful in algebra and beyond (IES 2010). Many of the models and contexts that are used to support students' early understanding of fraction concepts become problematic as students begin to perform computations with fractions. Although it may be reasonable to expect a student to understand the mathematics of adding $\frac{2}{3}$ to $\frac{5}{6}$ when thinking about pizza, making sense of multiplying $\frac{2}{3}$ by $\frac{5}{6}$ given the same context is difficult at best. Understanding that fractions are numbers that are part of the system of rational numbers and are ruled by the same mathematical properties as whole numbers and integers is a core aspect of having "fraction sense."

The Common Core State Standards for Mathematics provides the following definition of fractions:

> Understand a fraction 1/b as the quantity formed by 1 part when a whole is partitioned into b equal parts; understand a fraction a/b as the quantity formed by a parts of size 1/b. (2010, 24)

Unpacking this definition can be challenging for adults and even more so for students, so it is not at all surprising that instruction in fractions makes liberal use of representations and contexts intended to simplify the concept for students. Unfortunately, sometimes when simplifying the concept we inadvertently mask the underlying meaning of fractions (Armstrong and Larson 1995; Davydov and Tsetkovich 1992; Lamon 2007; Mack 1990, 1995). Hung-Hsi Wu, a mathematics professor emeritus at the University of California at Berkeley, has written extensively about the teaching and learning of fractions (Wu 1999, 2001, 2002, 2011). According to Wu,

> [i]n mathematics, do whatever it takes to help you learn something, provided you do not lose sight of what you are supposed to learn. In the case of fractions, it means you may use any pictorial image you want to process your thoughts on fractions, but at the end, you should be able to formulate logical arguments in terms of the original definition of a fraction as a point on the number line. (emphasis in original; 2002, 13)

In a conference talk about the development of students' understanding of whole numbers, Kathy Richardson (2008) suggested that students initially learn about whole numbers as *adjectives* or descriptors—students consider five *bears*, seven *cookies*, twenty-five *children*—the numbers are tied to specific contexts and examples. It is only after repeated experience, reflection, and opportunities to reason about numbers that students come to understand them as *nouns*, or concepts that can be manipulated regardless of context or setting. They understand 25 as a number between 24

> **It is only after repeated experience, reflection, and opportunities to reason about numbers that students come to understand them as nouns, or concepts that can be manipulated regardless of context or setting.**

and 26, as half of 50 and $\frac{1}{5}$ of 125, as 5^2 and 10 less than 35. All these things are true about the number 25 whether you're talking about 25 dogs, 25 dollars, 25 people, 25 anything.

I've extended this idea into the learning of fractions. It makes complete sense to me that we first teach fractions as adjectives—$\frac{1}{2}$ of a pizza, $\frac{3}{4}$ of an hour, $\frac{2}{3}$ of a cup. Then, like with whole numbers, students need opportunities to transition to considering fractions as *nouns* or concepts. Take $\frac{5}{8}$, for example. Students need to understand that $\frac{5}{8}$ is a little more than $\frac{1}{2}$ but less than $\frac{3}{4}$. It's $\frac{3}{8}$ less than 1, it is equivalent to $\frac{10}{16}$, it is two times $\frac{5}{16}$, it is half of $1\frac{1}{4}$, and so on. All these things are true about $\frac{5}{8}$ regardless of context, notation (fraction or decimal notation), or referent.

> **For students to compute with fractions *with understanding*, they must understand that fractions are numbers.**

For students to compute with fractions *with understanding*, they must understand that fractions are numbers. The following foundational understandings about fractions guide all the work in subsequent chapters. You may find it helpful to revisit this list from time to time as you continue to support students as they learn to compute with fractions.

FOUNDATIONAL UNDERSTANDINGS ABOUT FRACTIONS

- Fractions are numbers that operate under the same rules and properties as other rational numbers.
- The unit fraction is the building block of fractions.
- Fractions can be decomposed and recomposed in infinite ways.
- Equivalent fractions represent different ways of naming the same value.
- All rational numbers can be expressed as fractions in the form $\frac{a}{b}$, where b does not equal zero.

"It may be surprising that, for most students, to think of a rational number as a number—as an individual entity or a single point on a number line—is a novel idea" (National Research Council 2001, 235). Surprisingly, I have found this also to be a novel idea for many classroom teachers.

As part of a larger study examining students' understanding of fraction concepts and teachers' strategies for teaching fractions, my colleague and I asked teachers to respond to the following questions:

Darrell and Jerome are talking about fractions.

Darrell says that $\frac{1}{3}$ and $\frac{2}{6}$ are equivalent fractions.

Jerome says that $\frac{1}{3}$ and $\frac{2}{6}$ are the same number.

1. Who do you agree with?

   A. Darrell
   B. Jerome
   C. Both Darrell and Jerome
   D. Disagree with both Darrell and Jerome

2. How might you help students understand the answer to this problem?

The correct answer to this question is "C. Both Darrell and Jerome." Equivalent fractions, such as $\frac{1}{3}$ and $\frac{2}{6}$, occupy the same point on the number line, thus they are in fact the same number. Of the twenty-four teachers who responded to the question, more than half agreed with Darrell only, citing reasons such as, "They take up the same amount of space, but clearly they aren't the same number," and "They are similar fractions because they are the same amount BUT not same # b/c have different # of pieces" (emphasis included in original response). This is certainly a small sample of teachers, but in my work with teachers throughout the country, I have found similar responses. In addition, the strategies presented in response to question 2—How might you help students understand the answer to this problem?—often involved either references to food items, such as cake or pie, or parts of circular areas (see examples that follow).

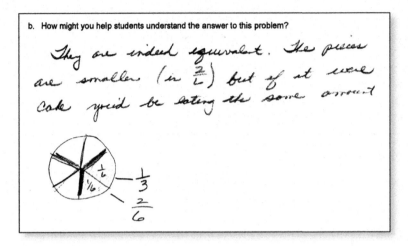

b. How might you help students understand the answer to this problem?

They are indeed equivalent. The pieces are smaller (in $\frac{2}{6}$) but if it were cake you'd be eating the same amount

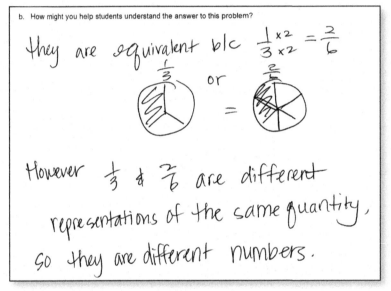

b. How might you help students understand the answer to this problem?

they are equivalent b/c $\frac{1 \times 2}{3 \times 2} = \frac{2}{6}$

However $\frac{1}{3}$ & $\frac{2}{6}$ are different representations of the same quantity, so they are different numbers.

    This is not to say that these teachers didn't understand that fractions could be representations of numbers, but it does indicate a hesitancy to consider fractions beyond visual and contextual representations. As the title of my other book, *Beyond Pizzas & Pies: 10 Essential Strategies for Supporting Fraction Sense, Grades 3–5, Second Edition* (McNamara and Shaughnessy 2015), implies, moving beyond such a limited conception of fractions is an essential aspect of acquiring a deep understanding of fractions.

Classroom Activities

1.1 *Add It Up*, Version 1

Overview

In this activity, students take hops on a number line to arrive at the number 1. Students also record equations showing how the number 1 can be represented as the sum of unit fractions.

Materials

Add It Up, Version 1, recording sheets (**Reproducible 1a**), 1 per student

die, 1 per pair of students labeled $\frac{1}{2}, \frac{1}{3}, \frac{1}{4}, \frac{1}{4}, \frac{1}{6}, \frac{1}{6}$

1. Pass out the fraction die, one per pair of students, as well as the *Add It Up*, Version 1 recording sheets, one per student. (See Figure 1–1; also available as Reproducible 1a.)

2. Tell students they will be using the recording sheet and die to play a game, the goal of which is to be the first person to get to the number 1 on each number line on their recording sheet.

3. Model the game, demonstrating for students how to roll the die and record both their hops on the number line and the resulting equation below the number line.

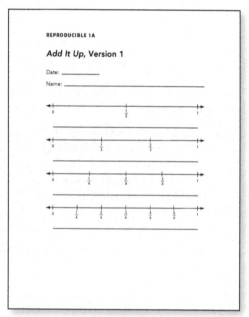

Figure 1–1. *Add It Up*, Version 1, recording sheet

Management Tip

Keeping dice contained and quiet can be challenging. Felt squares (available at your local craft store) or shoe box tops greatly reduce sound and travel.

4. To determine who goes first, players take turns rolling the die. The player who rolls the number closest to 1 goes first.

5. Player 1 rolls the die and uses the fraction shown on the die to determine on which number line to start. For example, if Player 1 rolls $\frac{1}{2}$, then she begins at 0 on the number line partitioned into halves and draws an arc to show a "hop" to $\frac{1}{2}$ as shown here. Player 1 also records the unit fraction she rolled below the appropriate number line.

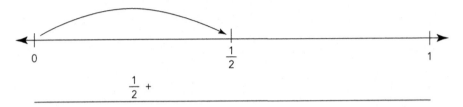

6. Play continues with Player 2 rolling the die, determining where to start, and recording both his hops and his fraction on his recording sheet.

7. On a player's second roll, he or she will either start at 0 on a new number line or, if the fraction rolled is the same as the first roll, will start where he or she hopped to on the first roll. For example, if Player 1 rolls $\frac{1}{2}$ again, she would start at $\frac{1}{2}$ and draw a hop from $\frac{1}{2}$ to 1, as shown here. She would also complete the equation below the line by writing $\frac{1}{2} + \frac{1}{2} = \frac{2}{2} = 1$.

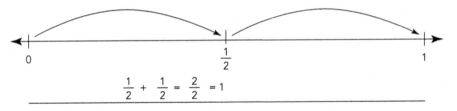

8. Play continues as players take turns rolling the die, recording their hops on the appropriate number line, and writing their rolls below the number line. If a player rolls a fraction he no longer needs, such as $\frac{1}{2}$ in the example of Player 1, he may roll again.

9. Play continues until one of the players makes it to 1 on all four number lines and has written all the accompanying equations below the lines.

1.2 Add It Up, Version 2

Materials

Add It Up, Version 2, recording sheets (**Reproducible 1b**), 1 per student

die, 1 per pair of students labeled $\frac{1}{2}, \frac{1}{3}, \frac{1}{4}, \frac{1}{6}, \frac{1}{8}, \frac{1}{12}$

Overview

Similar to *Add It Up*, Version 1, students take hops on a number line to arrive at 1. Students also record equations showing how the number 1 can be represented as the sum of unit fractions. In addition, students use their knowledge of equivalent fractions to make it to 1 on their number lines.

1. Pass out the fraction die, one per pair of students, as well as the *Add It Up*, Version 2 recording sheets, one per student. (See Figure 1–2; also available as Reproducible 1b.)

2. Tell students that, just like in *Add It Up*, Version 1, they will again be using the recording sheet and die to play a game, the goal of which is to be the first person to get to 1 on each number line on their recording sheet.

3. Explain there are two main differences between Version 1 and Version 2 of *Add It Up*. The first difference between Version 1 and Version 2 is the use of a different die and the addition of two more number lines, one partitioned into eighths and one partitioned into twelfths.

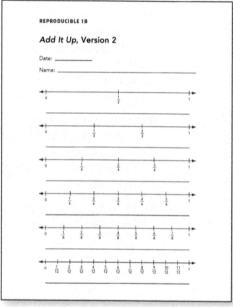

Figure 1–2. *Add It Up*, Version 2, recording sheet

4. The other difference is that after rolling the die, instead of having to use the same number line as shown on the die, in Version 2, students decide which number line to use. For example, if a student rolls $\frac{1}{4}$, he can decide whether he wants to hop on the number line partitioned into fourths or whether he wants to use another

This illustrates Strategy #3 of the ten essential strategies for supporting fraction sense: *Provide opportunities for students to recognize equivalent fractions as different ways to name the same quantity.* To learn more about this strategy, see Chapter 1 of *Beyond Pizzas & Pies: 10 Essential Strategies for Supporting Fraction Sense, Grades 3–5, Second Edition* (McNamara and Shaughnessy 2015).

line that has a fraction equivalent to one-fourth. An example that shows a way to get to $\frac{12}{12}$ with the rolls $\frac{1}{12}$, $\frac{1}{12}$, $\frac{1}{2}$, $\frac{1}{4}$, and $\frac{1}{12}$ is shown here.

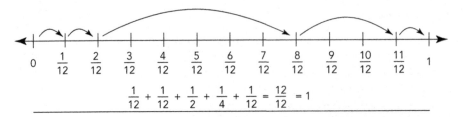

$$\frac{1}{12} + \frac{1}{12} + \frac{1}{2} + \frac{1}{4} + \frac{1}{12} = \frac{12}{12} = 1$$

5. Model the game, demonstrating for students how to roll the die and record both their hops on the number line and the resulting equation below the number line.

6. Play continues as in Version 1. If a player rolls a fraction she no longer needs, she may use it on another number or roll again.

Teaching Suggestion

As you model Version 2, think aloud how to decide where to start. For example, if you roll $\frac{1}{4}$, you might say, "I know I can use the one-fourth line, but I can also use the one-eighth line because two-eighths equals one-fourth, or I can use the one-twelfth line because three-twelfths equals one-fourth."

7. Play continues until one of the players completes all six number lines and has written all the accompanying equations below the lines.

Fractions Greater Than 1

Materials

Fractions Greater Than 1 recording sheet (**Reproducible 1c**), 1 per pair of students

Fraction Cards, Set A (**Reproducible 1d**), 1 set per group

Cuisenaire rods, 1 set per pair of students

Jumbo Cuisenaire rods or tag board "rods" with magnetic tape for display

sentence strips, 1 per pair of students

glue sticks, 1 per pair of students

Overview

In this activity, students work with a partner to place fractions and mixed numbers greater than 1 on a number line. They also focus on equivalency.

Manipulative Note

Cuisenaire rods are wooden or plastic blocks that range in length from 1 to 10 cm. Each rod of a given length is the same color. That is, all the 1-cm rods are white, all the 2-cm rods are red, all the 3-cm rods are light green, and so on.

1. Display a large number line with the numbers 0 to 4 marked as shown here. If using the Jumbo Cuisenaire rods or a homemade equivalent, your unit interval should be 24 cm.

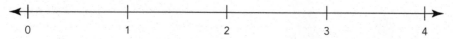

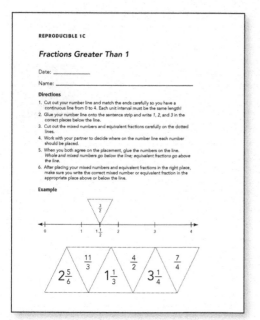

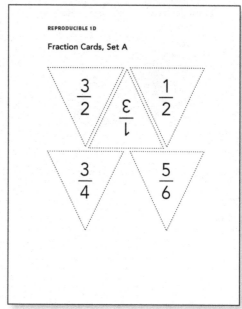

Figure 1–3. *Fractions Greater Than 1 and Fractions Cards, Set A*

2. Show students the $\frac{1}{2}$ card and ask for a volunteer to come up and place it on the number line. (See Figure 1–3 on page 15; also available as Reproducible 1d.)

3. Ask the student to justify his or her placement and invite the other students to provide feedback about the placement. For example, if students don't agree with the placement, ask them to explain why and to help the other student find the correct placement.

4. Repeat with the cards showing $\frac{1}{3}$, $\frac{3}{4}$, and $\frac{5}{6}$.

This illustrates Strategy #9 of the ten essential strategies for supporting fraction sense: *Provide opportunities for students to engage in mathematical discourse and share and discuss their mathematical ideas, even those that may not be fully formed or completely accurate.* To learn more about this strategy, see Chapter 1 of *Beyond Pizzas & Pies: 10 Essential Strategies for Supporting Fraction Sense, Grades 3–5, Second Edition* (McNamara and Shaughnessy 2015).

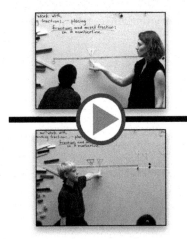

VIDEO CLIP 1a

Placing $\frac{1}{2}$ on the Number Line

This clip comes at the beginning of Activity 1.3. After Ms. Kretschmar shows students a four-unit number line with only the whole numbers 0 and 4 labeled, we see several students share their thinking about where to place $\frac{1}{2}$ on the line. Three different locations are suggested and discussed. What does Ms. Kretschmar learn about what students do and don't understand about fractions on the number line from the discussion?

To view this video clip, scan the QR code or access via http://hein.pub/MathOLR

For commentary on the above, see the Appendix: Author's Video Reflections.

VIDEO CLIP 1b

Using Cuisenaire Rods to Place $\frac{1}{3}$ on the Number Line

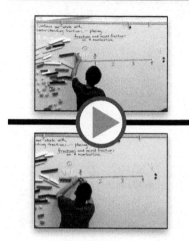

In this clip, we see two students, Coleo and Juan, show where $\frac{1}{3}$ goes on the number line. Why does Ms. Kretschmar call on Juan to use the Cuisenaire rods to justify Coleo's placement? How does Juan's use of the Cuisenaire rods support students' understanding of placing fractions on the number line?

To view this video clip, scan the QR code or access via http://hein.pub/MathOLR

For commentary on the above, see the Appendix: Author's Video Reflections.

5. Make sure to be explicit about how to use the Cuisenaire rods to partition the unit interval into the appropriate number of segments. For example, with the fraction $\frac{1}{3}$, guide students to the understanding that the unit interval needs to be partitioned into three equal segments because the denominator of the fraction is three. If you find your students are really struggling with this, you may want to teach one of the number line lessons from Chapter 2 in *Beyond Pizzas & Pies, Second Edition* (NcNamara and Shaughnessy 2015), *before* doing this activity.

6. Show students $\frac{2}{3}$ and ask for a volunteer to come up and place it on the number line.

7. Ask the student to justify her placement and invite the other students to provide feedback about the placement. For example, if students don't agree with the placement, ask them to explain why and to help the other student find the correct placement.

Figure 1–4. Example of student-made number line from Activity 1.3.

Using Cuisenaire Rods to Place $\frac{3}{2}$ on the Number Line

In this clip, we see Samantha place $\frac{3}{2}$ on the number line. How does Samantha use the Cuisenaire rods to help her place the fraction?

To view this video clip, scan the QR code or access via http://hein.pub/MathOLR

For commentary on the above, see the Appendix: Author's Video Reflections.

8. Ask students what is different about the fraction $\frac{3}{2}$ compared with the other fraction they placed on the line.

9. Students will notice the fraction is between 1 and 2, unlike the other fractions, which were all less than 1 (or between 0 and 1).

10. Tell students that they are going to work with a partner and use the Cuisenaire rods to place fractions on a number line and that all of the fractions are greater than 1.

11. Give students the recording sheet and answer questions about the task. (See Figure 1–5; also available as Reproducible 1d.) Students may take turns placing numbers but have to explain their rationale to their partner.

12. Remind students that improper fractions should be placed above the line and mixed numbers should be placed below the line. After placing the numbers, students should write the mixed number or improper fraction equivalent in the appropriate place.

13. After students have placed all their fractions, have them compare their results with another pair of students and discuss any discrepancies.

14. Wrap up the lesson by asking students to share their strategies for translating between mixed numbers and improper fractions.

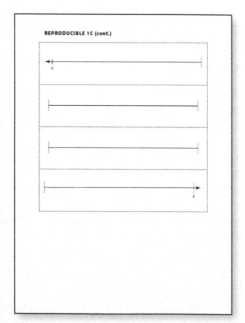

Figure 1–5. *Fractions Greater Than 1* recording sheet

VIDEO CLIP 1d

Deciding Where to Place $\frac{11}{3}$ on the Number Line

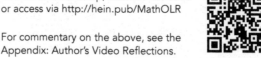

In this clip, we hear from Braulio as he shares how he and his partner determined where to place $\frac{11}{3}$. How does Braulio draw on his understanding of unit fractions and whole numbers to decide which two whole numbers $\frac{11}{3}$ is between?

To view this video clip, scan the QR code or access via http://hein.pub/MathOLR

For commentary on the above, see the Appendix: Author's Video Reflections.

1.4 One Number, Many Names

Materials

Fraction Cards, Set B (**Reproducible 1e**), 1 set per group

timer or clock with a second hand

Overview

This activity should follow students' experiences with explicit lessons focused on creating equivalent fractions using concrete and pictorial representations of fractions. As students name a given fraction in as many ways as possible in the allotted time, they build their fluency with equivalent fractions. This fluency will support them as they use their knowledge of equivalency to add and subtract fractions. This activity can be done with the whole class, as a partner activity, or as an independent activity if students have access to a timer.

1. Prepare the fraction cards. (See Figure 1–6; also available as Reproducible 1e.) Begin by asking students to write down all the ways they can think of to write the number 1 as a fraction.

2. Students are likely to begin by writing $\frac{2}{2}$, $\frac{3}{3}$, $\frac{4}{4}$, $\frac{5}{5}$, $\frac{6}{6}$, and so on. After several seconds have passed, ask who thinks they have all the possible answers.

3. Depending on your students, the notion that there are infinite possibilities may not be stated explicitly. Most students, however, will realize that the list could go on for a very long time.

4. Ask for volunteers to share one of their names for the number 1 as a fraction and explain how they know it belongs on the list. If students have trouble providing a rationale for their answer, you may want to suggest they think about work they have done with fraction kits, number lines, and other materials. Encourage students to justify their answer by saying something such as, "two-halves is one-half plus one-half" or "two-halves is two copies of one-half."

This illustrates Strategy #3 of the ten essential strategies for supporting fraction sense: *Provide opportunities for students to recognize equivalent fractions as different ways to name the same quantity.* To learn more about this strategy, see Chapter 1 of *Beyond Pizzas & Pies: 10 Essential Strategies for Supporting Fraction Sense, Grades 3–5, Second Edition* (McNamara and Shaughnessy 2015).

5. Allow several more volunteers to share, always asking them to justify their answers.

6. Tell students that when they provide alternative names for the same number, they are not changing the value of the number, but instead are *renaming* the number. Explain that *equivalent fractions* are *renamed fractions*. Although the numbers used as the numerator and denominator are different, the value of the fraction remains the same.

7. Explain to students they are going to do the same thing with another fraction, but this time you will use a timer to give them a set amount of time to rename the fraction. The purpose of the timer is not to make students feel pressured or rushed, but to keep the number of possibilities students write manageable.

8. Show students the $\frac{1}{2}$ card. Start the timer and tell them to write as many names as they can for one-half.

9. After the timer goes off, have students share their lists with a partner, adding any new names for one-half to their list. After a few minutes of partner talk, ask for volunteers to share and justify their answers with the whole class.

10. Continue with other fractions, allowing students to share and justify their answers as time permits.

11. The fractions on the cards are suggestions for use. You can easily differentiate this activity by selecting the fractions you ask students to rename.

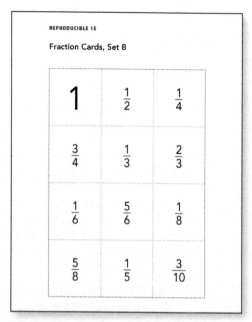

REPRODUCIBLE 1E

Fraction Cards, Set B

1	$\frac{1}{2}$	$\frac{1}{4}$
$\frac{3}{4}$	$\frac{1}{3}$	$\frac{2}{3}$
$\frac{1}{6}$	$\frac{5}{6}$	$\frac{1}{8}$
$\frac{5}{8}$	$\frac{1}{5}$	$\frac{3}{10}$

Figure 1–6. Fraction Cards, Set B

Which Does Not Belong?

Materials
none

Overview

Which Does Not Belong? is a routine that can be used throughout the year with any content. Students are shown four to five images (they could be numbers, shapes, expressions, words, and so on) and are asked to select one that is different from the others. At first, students' responses may be somewhat shallow and based on surface-level differences, but as students engage in *Which Does Not Belong?*, over time their rationales for selecting the image that does not belong become more insightful.

This illustrates Strategy #8 of the ten essential strategies for supporting fraction sense: *Provide students with multiple strategies for comparing and reasoning about fractions.* **To learn more about this strategy, see Chapter 1 of Beyond Pizzas & Pies: 10 Essential Strategies for Supporting Fraction Sense, Grades 3–5, Second Edition (McNamara and Shaughnessy 2015).**

1. Display the following fractions where all students can see them:

$$\frac{1}{2}, \frac{7}{14}, \frac{5}{3}, \frac{6}{12}$$

2. Ask students to look at the four fractions and select one that they think does not belong with the rest.

3. Assure students there is not one correct answer, and allow time for them to think on their own, possibly jotting down their reason for choosing the fraction.

4. For students who choose quickly, suggest they select another fraction and determine why it could be the one that doesn't belong.

5. Ask for volunteers to share which fraction they think doesn't belong and why. After students share, be sure to ask whether anyone else chose the same fraction but for a different reason.

6. Reasons that each fraction might be chosen include the following:

   $\frac{1}{2}$: It's the only unit fraction.

   $\frac{7}{14}$: It's the only fraction with a denominator that is not a factor of twelve.

   $\frac{5}{3}$: It's the only fraction greater than one; it's the only fraction not equal to one-half.

   $\frac{6}{12}$: It's the only fraction that has an even number as the numerator; it's the only fraction that has an even number for both the numerator and the denominator.

7. After students have exhausted the reasons for the four fractions shown, show another set of fractions and repeat the process.

$$\frac{2}{3}, \frac{2}{8}, \frac{2}{4}, \frac{4}{20}$$

8. Reasons that each fraction might be chosen include the following:

$\frac{2}{3}$: It's the only fraction that can't be renamed as a unit fraction.

$\frac{2}{8}$: It's the only fraction equivalent to one-fourth.

$\frac{2}{4}$: It's the only fraction equivalent to one-half.

$\frac{4}{20}$: It's the only fraction equivalent to one-fifth.

$$\frac{21}{7}, \frac{10}{3}, \frac{12}{4}, \frac{18}{3}$$

9. Here is another set of fractions to show, followed by reasons that each fraction might be chosen.

$\frac{21}{7}$: It's the only fraction with an odd numerator and denominator.

$\frac{10}{3}$: It's the only fraction that can't be renamed as a whole number.

$\frac{12}{4}$: It's the only fraction with an even numerator and denominator.

$\frac{18}{3}$: It's the only fraction that can be renamed as 6; it's the only fraction that can be renamed as a number greater than three and one-third.

The understanding that fractions are numbers that can be decomposed and recomposed prepares students for later work with fraction computation. When students know that three-fourths is made up of three one-fourths, they are building the foundation for understanding fraction addition and subtraction—$\frac{1}{4} + \frac{1}{4} + \frac{1}{4} = \frac{3}{4}$ and $\frac{3}{4} - \frac{1}{4} = \frac{2}{4}$, as well as multiplication and division: $3 \times \frac{1}{4} = \frac{3}{4}$ (and $\frac{1}{4} \times 3 = \frac{3}{4}$); $\frac{3}{4} \div 3 = \frac{1}{4}$ and $\frac{3}{4} \div \frac{1}{4} = 3$. In addition, understanding that equivalent fractions are different ways of naming the same number is essential as students transform (or "rename") fractions when adding and subtracting fractions with unlike denominators. More information and classroom activities on the topic of addition and subtraction can be found in Chapters 2 through 4, and multiplication and division in Chapters 5 through 7.

Study Questions

After Reading Chapter 1

1. What information presented in the "Classroom Scenario," "What's the Math?" and "What's the Research?" sections was familiar to you or similar to your experience with students?

2. Understanding fractions as numbers represents a somewhat different focus for fraction instruction than we've seen in the past. How will this influence how you approach fractions instruction with your students?

3. Which of the Classroom Activities (Activity 1.1, *Add It Up*, Version 1; Activity 1.2, *Add It Up*, Version 2; Activity 1.3, *Fractions Greater Than One*; Activity 1.4, *One Number, Many Names*; or Activity 1.5, *Which Does Not Belong?*) do you plan to implement with your students?

After Trying One or More of the Activities

1. Describe the activity and any modifications you made to meet your students' needs or to align with your curriculum.

2. How did this activity add to your knowledge of what your students do and do not understand about fractions as numbers?

3. What are your next steps for supporting your students' learning about fractions as numbers?

Connections to *Beyond Pizzas & Pies, Second Edition*

Beyond Invert & Multiply builds on the foundational understandings introduced in its companion resource, *Beyond Pizzas & Pies: 10 Essential Strategies for Supporting Fraction Sense, Grades 3–5, Second Edition*. I recommend pairing this chapter with Chapters 3 and 8 in *Beyond Pizzas & Pies, Second Edition*, to continue your learning.

Addition and Subtraction with Fractions

Developing Awareness

Addition and Subtraction Problem Types

Understanding addition and subtraction involves more than just the ability to find the sum or difference accurately when presented with a corresponding equation. It also involves being able to make sense of mathematical situations to determine which operation is called for, and then knowing what the resulting answers represent. For example, given the problem *A captain owns 26 sheep and 10 goats. How old is the captain?*, students often provide the answer of 36, even though it makes no sense given the context of the problem (Verschaffel, Greer, and de Corte 2000). This answer indicates that students have a problem not with the calculation involved, because 26 plus 10 does, indeed, equal 36, but instead with the act of doing the calculation at all. The context of the problem does not call for any calculation to be performed; however, most teachers have no problem predicting this response because they've seen their own students do similar things when presented with word problems containing two or more terms.

Before students in the early grades are asked to solve whole number addition and subtraction problems without contexts, they are given multiple opportunities to consider what the operations mean. These opportunities typically take the form of word problems, such as, *Our class has 14 girls and 12 boys. How many students are in our class?* or, *Our class has 26 students. 12 of them are boys. How many students in our class are girls?* Problems like this make sense to students and can be easily represented with manipulative materials, drawings, or the actual students themselves. However, in order for students to solve these types of problems correctly, it is essential that they understand what the problems are about. It is not enough that they are able to compute correctly; they must also interpret the problem situation to determine which operation is called for. For example, a student who misinterprets the problem *Our class has 26 students. 12 of them are boys. How many students in our class are girls?* by adding 26 and 12 to arrive at an answer of 38, does not have a problem with computation, but instead with making sense of the problem as written. In order for students to become "mathematically proficient" as called for in the Standards for Mathematical Practice (NGA Center/CCSSO 2010) they need to develop their facility with solving decontextualized calculations and interpreting contextualized problems. The two aspects of proficiency described here: (1) the ability to compute accurately and efficiently and (2) the ability to interpret problem situations correctly, develop in tandem, each being supported by and supporting the other. As students' understanding of whole numbers and operations develops, and their strategies for solving addition and subtraction problems develop, they no longer need to consider the context of a problem to determine if 26 is a reasonable answer to the problem *14 + 12*.

Just like with whole numbers, as students learn to make sense of fractions as numbers and consider the reasonableness of the results of fraction computation, contexts can provide meaningful supports. Knowing the different types of situations that can be solved with addition and subtraction, and incorporating these problem types into your instruction, is instrumental in helping your students learn to solve fraction addition and subtraction problems accurately, efficiently, and with understanding.

> Just like with whole numbers, as students learn to make sense of fractions as numbers and consider the reasonableness of the results of fraction computation, contexts can provide meaningful supports.

Problem Types: Addition and Subtraction

A great deal of research has gone into identifying types of addition and subtraction situations as well as how students approach different problem types (Carpenter, Fennema, Franke, Levi, and Empson 1999). Table 2–1 presents the different problem types.

Table 2–1. Addition and Subtraction Problem Types

	Start unknown	Change unknown	Result unknown
Join (also called Add To)	Some teachers are in the staff room. Three more teachers come into the room. Now there are seven teachers in the staff room. *How many teachers were there before?*	Four teachers are in the staff room. Some more teachers come into the room. Now there are seven teachers in the staff room. *How many teachers came into the staff room?*	Four teachers are in the staff room. Three more teachers come into the room. *How many teachers are in the staff room?*
Separate (also called Take From)	There are some teachers in the staff room. Three of them leave. Now there are four teachers in the staff room. *How many teachers were there before?*	There were seven teachers in the staff room. Some teachers leave, so now there are four teachers in the staff room. *How many teachers left the staff room?*	There are seven teachers in the staff room. Three teachers leave. *How many teachers are in the staff room now?*

	Part unknown	Whole unknown
Part–Part–Whole (also called Put together/ Take apart)	Some math specialists and three science specialists are in a meeting. There are seven specialists in the meeting. *How many math specialists are in the meeting?* Four math specialists and some science specialists are in a meeting. There are seven specialists in the meeting. *How many science specialists are in the meeting?*	Four math specialists and three science specialists are in a meeting. *How many specialists are in the meeting?*

Table 2–1. *(cont.)*

	Difference unknown	Quantity unknown	Referent unknown
Compare	I spent six hours grading papers this weekend. My grade-level partner spent eight hours grading papers. *How much more time did my partner spend grading than I did?*	I spent six hours grading papers this weekend. My grade-level partner spent two hours more than I did grading papers. *How much time did my partner spend grading papers?*	I spent six hours grading papers this weekend. I spent two fewer hours grading than my grade-level partner did. *How much time did my partner spend grading papers?*

Source: Adapted from Carpenter, Fennema, Franke, Levi, and Empson (1999, p. 12).

Among addition and subtraction there are four main situations: *join* (also called *add to*), *separate* (also called *take from*), *part–part–whole* (also called *put together/take apart*), and *compare*.

Within each of the four situations, any one of the numbers involved (the start, the change, or the result) could be the unknown. For example, given the following *join* situation, *Four teachers are in the staff room. Three more teachers come into the room. Now there are seven teachers in the staff room*, changing the unknown results in the following three problems:

JOIN SITUATION

1. *Result unknown:* Four teachers are in the staff room. Three more teachers come into the room. *How many teachers are in the staff room?*

2. *Change unknown:* Four teachers are in the staff room. Some more teachers come into the room. Now there are seven teachers in the staff room. *How many teachers came into the staff room?*

3. *Start unknown:* Some teachers are in the staff room. Three more teachers come into the room. Now there are seven teachers in the staff room. *How many teachers were there before?*

Interestingly, although different problem situations may be solved with the same calculation, the context of the problem can make it easier or more difficult for students to solve. Take the problem just described. As a *join* situation, the context has an implied action—one can imagine the four teachers in the room, the three teachers joining them, and the resulting seven teachers. The problem is represented easily by using manipulatives such as counters or tiles, and it can also be shown using tally marks or a number line. In contrast, the following *part–part–whole* situation, although solved using the same equations, is more challenging for students because there is no implied action: *There are four math specialists and three science specialists in a meeting. There are seven specialists in the meeting in all.* In this case, the four math specialists and three science specialists (the parts) comprise the larger static set of specialists (the group). No one comes or goes; hence, the following three problems do not involve any action that students can represent easily:

PART–PART–WHOLE SITUATION: STARTING WITH THE PART

1. *Result unknown:* Four math specialists and three science specialists are in a meeting. *How many specialists are in the meeting?*
2. *Change unknown:* Four math specialists and some science specialists are in a meeting. There are seven specialists in the meeting. *How many science specialists are in the meeting?*
3. *Start unknown:* Some math specialists and three science specialists are in a meeting. There are seven specialists in the meeting. *How many math specialists are in the meeting?*

In addition to the type of situation influencing the difficulty level of the problems, which value is the unknown also affects problem difficulty. In both of the previous situations, problems in which the result is unknown are the easiest for students to solve, followed by change unknown, with start-unknown problems generally the most challenging.

It may be obvious that both of the two problem situations just described could be rewritten slightly as *separate* or subtraction *part–part–whole* problems, respectively. Given the first situation of teachers in the staff room, when written by starting with the result, *There are seven teachers in the staff room. Three teachers leave. Now there are four teachers in the staff room,* the resulting three *separate* problems are as follows:

SEPARATE SITUATION

1. *Result unknown:* There are seven teachers in the staff room. Three teachers leave. *How many teachers are in the staff room now?*
2. *Change unknown:* There were seven teachers in the staff room. Some teachers leave, so now there are four teachers in the staff room. *How many teachers left the staff room?*
3. *Start unknown:* There are some teachers in the staff room. Three of them leave. Now there are four teachers in the staff room. *How many teachers were there before?*

The *part–part–whole* situation can be rewritten as follows: *There are seven specialists in the meeting. Four are math specialists and three are science specialists.* The resulting three problems are as follows:

PART–PART–WHOLE SITUATION: STARTING WITH THE WHOLE

1. *Result unknown:* There are seven specialists in a meeting. Four of them are math specialists and the rest of them are science specialists. *How many science specialists are in the meeting?*

2. *Change unknown:* There are seven specialists in a meeting. Some of them are math specialists and three of them are science specialists. *How many math specialists are in the meeting?*

3. *Start unknown:* Some specialists are in a meeting. Four of them are math specialists and three of them are science specialists. *How many specialists are in the meeting?*

In addition, *part–part–whole* problems can be written with both parts unknown, resulting in many correct answers. For example, *There are seven specialists in a meeting. Some are math specialists and some are science specialists. How many of each could there be?*

COMPARE SITUATION

Among the most challenging problem situations for students to solve are *compare* situations. Unlike *join* and *separate* situations, with *compare* situations there is no implied action. *Compare* situations often include terms such as *fewer* and *more than*, and ask questions such as "How many more?" and "How many fewer?" (NGA Center/CCSSO 2010). Students often find it very difficult to interpret *compare* problems and determine which operation to use to solve them. In addition to the difficulties students may have with interpreting the language of *compare* problems, students may also be told by textbooks and teachers to solve a problem such as, *I spent six hours grading papers this weekend. My grade-level partner spent eight hours grading papers. How many more hours did my partner spend than I did?*, by using subtraction (8 – 6), when it makes more sense to many students to solve by considering the problem as a missing addend problem (6 + ? = 8) and either count up or rely on known facts to get the answer. Both strategies result in the same answer of two, but the problem as written does not imply take-away.

In Summary

Although the research on addition and subtraction problem types, and students' approaches to solving them, is based on work with whole numbers, the same ideas apply when students transition to computations with fractions. When presenting students with contextualized fraction addition and subtraction problems (or word problems), it is just as important to consider the problem situations to which students are exposed, as it is when students are working with whole numbers. Students need opportunities to grapple with and make sense of various problem types and to interpret the results of their calculations. It is important to keep in mind (1) there are many different types of problem situations, (2) students find different types of problem situations more or less difficult to solve, and (3) many subtraction problems may be solved more easily as missing addend problems.

Contexts can support students to understand the meaning of addition and subtraction of fractions, and to help them consider the reasonableness of their results (Dixon and Tobias 2013). Contexts that involve time and distance can be represented with linear models, such as Cuisenaire rods and number lines, to support students' understanding of fractions as numbers on the number line. In addition, researchers from the Rational Number Project have found that circle models can be used to support students' understanding of part–whole relations and the relative size of fractions (Cramer, Wyberg, and Leavitt 2008).

As with whole number computation, students need multiple opportunities to consider computation with fractions through solving a variety of problem types. Such opportunities enable students to approach fraction addition and subtraction from a sense-making point of view, instead of simply trying to compute without considering what the numbers in the problems mean. It is important to note that some of the problems in the following chapters are presented without contexts. This is not an oversight, but rather an intentional decision to provide opportunities for students to reason about fractions as numbers outside of a specific context. Although contexts can, and should, be used to help students to make sense of operations and to check their results for reasonableness, students ultimately need to be able to manipulate fractions and perform calculations context free. As stated in the Common Core State Standards for Mathematical Practice,

> Mathematically proficient students have . . . the ability to *decontextualize*— to abstract a given situation and represent it symbolically and manipulate the representing symbols as if they have a life of their own, without necessarily attending to their referents—and the ability to *contextualize*, to pause as needed during the manipulation process in order to probe into the referents for the symbols involved. (NGA/CCSSO 2010, 6)

Study Questions

After Reading Chapter 2

1. What information presented in the "What's the Context?" and "What's the Research?" sections was familiar to you or similar to your experience with students?

2. How might you use knowledge of different addition and subtraction problem types to support your students' understanding of addition and subtraction with fractions?

Making Sense
Addition with Fractions

OUTLINE

CCSS Connections

Prerequisite Standards

3.NF.A.1: Understand a fraction $1/b$ as the quantity formed by 1 part when a whole is partitioned into b equal parts; understand a fraction a/b as the quantity formed by [a] parts of size $1/b$.

3.NF.A.2: Understand a fraction as a number on the number line; represent fractions on a number line diagram.

Standards Addressed

4.NF.B.3: Understand a fraction a/b with $a > 1$ as a sum of fractions $1/b$.

4.NF.B.3a: Understand addition and subtraction of fractions as joining and separating parts referring to the same whole.

4.NF.B.3b: Decompose a fraction into a sum of fractions with the same denominator in more than one way, recording each decomposition by an equation. Justify decompositions, e.g., by using a visual fraction model.

4.NF.B.3c: Add and subtract mixed numbers with like denominators, e.g., by replacing each mixed number with an equivalent fraction, and/or by using properties of operations and the relationship between addition and subtraction.

5.NF.A.1: Add and subtract fractions with unlike denominators (including mixed numbers) by replacing given fractions with equivalent fractions in such a way as to produce an equivalent sum or difference of fractions with like denominators.

Mr. Gregory was looking forward to the lesson on adding proper fractions and mixed numbers that he had planned for his fifth graders. He knew that students often added across numerators and denominators, arriving at answers that made little sense. However, he had evidence that the work he had done with his class on using equivalent fractions to add fractions with unlike denominators had really paid off. His students rarely made the kinds of mistakes he heard other teachers talk about.

To get students warmed up after the weekend, he put a few problems on the board and told students to talk in their groups about the answers. As he circulated he heard students discussing their solutions, using the strategies they had been working on for the past several weeks.

"Five-sixths plus three-fourths? That's easy! You just got to make 'em both twelfths and then you can add 'em no problem!" Jerrell said confidently, as he wrote $\frac{10}{12} + \frac{9}{12} = \frac{19}{12}$ on his mini-white board.

"Yeah, Mr. G, give us something harder!" begged Lucia, always up for a challenge.

"Yeah, this stuff is too easy for us," Monique teased as her partner Samoa nodded.

"This is music to my ears," Mr. Gregory replied, smiling. "Try a few more of these just to get warmed up and then I'll throw something new at you." A few students pretended to duck as Mr. Gregory mimed throwing his marker.

The next problem Mr. Gregory presented, $2\frac{4}{5} + 3\frac{3}{10}$, was one that he felt sure his students would have little trouble with. However, as he circulated while students were working on the problem, he was surprised by what he saw. The majority of his students had incorrect answers to the problem. As he completed his first circuit of the classroom, he realized that their difficulties primarily took two forms. About half of the students added the whole numbers correctly but then reverted back to adding across numerators and denominators of the fractions, getting $5\frac{7}{15}$ for their answer, even though they had not done this on the previous problems. The other half of the students had no problem with the unlike denominators but completely ignored the whole numbers. Some of them renamed $\frac{4}{5}$ as $\frac{8}{10}$, then added $\frac{8}{10}$ to $\frac{3}{10}$ to get $\frac{11}{10}$ as their final answer. Others renamed $\frac{3}{10}$ as $\frac{1}{5}$ plus $\frac{1}{10}$, added $\frac{1}{5}$ to $\frac{4}{5}$ to get 1, then added on the remaining $\frac{1}{10}$, writing $1\frac{1}{10}$ as their final answer.

Before discussing the problem with the whole class, Mr. Gregory decided to give them another similar problem: $4\frac{5}{6} + 1\frac{3}{8}$. Before showing them the new problem he asked students to make sure not to erase their answer to $2\frac{4}{5} + 3\frac{3}{10}$. Sure enough, in response to the problem, students either wrote $5\frac{8}{14}$ or renamed the fractional parts of the problem correctly as $\frac{20}{24}$ and $\frac{9}{24}$, and ignored the whole numbers in the original problem when writing their answer.

As he called the class back together to discuss the problems, Mr. Gregory rewrote $2\frac{4}{5} + 3\frac{3}{10}$ on the board. He asked the students to look at the numbers that were being added and think about everything they knew about the answer. Mr. Gregory had introduced this routine earlier in the year when working with whole number multiplication and division but had not used it yet with fractions.

"I don't want you to tell me the answer; just tell me everything you know about the answer," he prompted.

After some time had passed, Mr. Gregory called on Constance to tell him something she knew about the answer.

"Well," she began, "it's going to be more than three, wait, more than four, or—yeah, more than five." Mr. Gregory saw that several students agreed with Constance.

"Constance, can you say more about that?" asked Mr. Gregory.

"If I've got two of something plus three more of something I will end up with at least five of something and the fractions will make it even more than that."

"Who has something else to add?"

"I think the answer will have a fraction in it because four-fifths plus three-tenths adds up to more than one," JT suggested. "There will be a little bit left over."

"Can someone rephrase what JT just said? I'm not sure everyone was following," Mr. Gregory asked, knowing many students were still mulling over Constance's idea about the answer being more than five and may have missed JT's important contribution about the answer not being a whole number.

"I think JT was saying that the two fractions in the answer will add up to more than one because four-fifths plus one-fifth equals one, and three-tenths is more than one-fifth," Lucia explained as JT nodded his agreement.

"So we have some important ideas out on the table right now. Constance told us that the answer will definitely be more than five because of the whole numbers in the problem. JT suggested that the answer will also have a fraction in it, because he was looking at the fractional parts of the two numbers being added." Mr. Gregory moved to the front of the room and wrote $5\frac{7}{15}$, $\frac{11}{10}$, and $1\frac{1}{10}$ on the board.

"Let's look at the three main answers I saw as I walked around the room. Talk at your tables about what you notice and see if you can figure out how people arrived at these answers."

As Mr. Gregory circulated and listened to the conversations at the tables he was pleased that students were able to identify the mistakes that resulted in the incorrect answers. He realized, however, that his students' understanding was not as robust as he had thought as evidenced by their challenges with the new problem types. As he thought about what to do next, he was reminded of how important it was to help students connect new problems and situations to concepts, strategies, and procedures that they already knew. He called the class back together and wrote $4\frac{5}{6} + 1\frac{3}{8}$ on the board.

"Tell me all you can about the answer to this problem," Mr. Gregory began.

S tudents' understanding of and strategies for addition of whole numbers has been well documented (Carpenter, Fennema, Franke, Levi, and Empson 1999). In the primary grades, students need opportunities to develop the understanding that whole numbers can be decomposed and recomposed in multiple ways; to use and become fluent with various strategies for adding numbers based on known facts, place value, and the properties of operations; to see the inverse relationship between addition and subtraction; and to solve problems representing a variety of problem types. As students move into the upper elementary grades and solve problems involving fractions, they need many opportunities to apply these understandings to addition of fractions and mixed numbers (NGA Center/ CCSSO 2010).

> **As students move into the upper elementary grades and solve problems involving fractions, they need many opportunities to apply these understandings to addition of fractions and mixed numbers.**

Decomposition

The understanding that a fraction can be decomposed into the sum of fractions in more than one way builds on students' understanding of unit fractions and fraction equivalency. For example, given a problem such as $\frac{2}{3} + \frac{2}{3}$, knowing that $\frac{2}{3}$ is made up of two $\frac{1}{3}$s (or $\frac{1}{3}$ plus $\frac{1}{3}$), allows one to add $\frac{2}{3}$ plus $\frac{1}{3}$ to get to 1, then to add the second $\frac{1}{3}$ to arrive at the answer of $1\frac{1}{3}$ (see the following illustration).

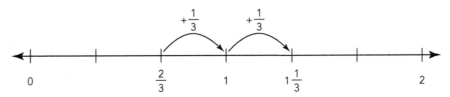

In addition, the understanding that $\frac{1}{3}$ is equivalent to $\frac{2}{6}$, allows one to add $\frac{5}{6}$ plus $\frac{1}{3}$ by first adding $\frac{5}{6}$ and $\frac{1}{6}$ to get to 1, then adding the second $\frac{1}{6}$ to arrive at the answer of $1\frac{1}{6}$ (see the following figure).

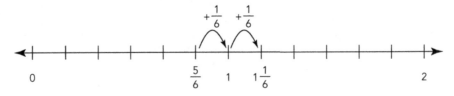

Commutative Property

The commutative property of addition makes it possible to add numbers in any order. Given a problem such as $\frac{1}{8} + \frac{7}{8}$, one may choose to reverse the addends and begin at $\frac{7}{8}$ and add $\frac{1}{8}$ instead of starting at $\frac{1}{8}$ and adding $\frac{7}{8}$.

Associative Property

The associative property of addition allows one to group addends in any way. For example, the problem $\frac{1}{4} + \frac{1}{2} + \frac{1}{2}$, can be solved by either grouping the first and second addend as $(\frac{1}{4} + \frac{1}{2}) + \frac{1}{2}$, or grouping the second and third addend: $\frac{1}{4} + (\frac{1}{2} + \frac{1}{2})$. Because of the associative property, either grouping results in the correct sum of $1\frac{1}{4}$; however, the second way, $\frac{1}{4} + (\frac{1}{2} + \frac{1}{2})$, is likely easier to solve.

When adding fractions, the commutative and associative properties are often used in conjunction with the decomposition strategy. (See the following example.)

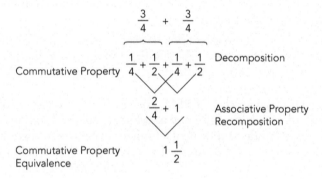

The Common Core State Standards for Mathematics (CCSSM) calls for grade 4 students to "Understand addition (and subtraction) of fractions as joining and separating parts referring to the same whole" and "Add and subtract mixed numbers with like denominators, e.g., by replacing each mixed number with an equivalent fraction, and/or by using properties of operations and the relationship between addition and subtraction" (NGA Center/CCSSO 2010, 30). (It is important to note that the text of the CCSSM does not include the use of the term *improper fractions*, but instead uses the term *equivalent fractions*.) In grade 5, students "Add and subtract fractions with unlike denominators (including mixed numbers) by replacing given fractions with equivalent fractions in such a way as to produce an equivalent sum or difference of fractions with like denominators" (36). For students to do this, it is necessary they understand that fractions can be decomposed into smaller fractions, and that equivalent fractions are merely different names for the same number or value. The classroom activities in this chapter focus on addition. For classroom activities on strategies for subtraction, see Chapter 4, Making Sense: Subtraction with Fractions, page 61.

S tudents' challenges with fraction computation are well known to teachers in the middle grades. A widely reported finding from the 1996 National Assessment of Education Progress test involves the response of thirteen-year-olds to the following item:

> Estimate the answer to $\frac{12}{13} + \frac{7}{8}$. You will not have time to solve the problem using paper and pencil.

The answer choices were *1, 2, 19, 21*, and *I don't know*. Only 24 percent of the students tested chose the correct answer of 2. This finding is disturbing for multiple reasons. One could draw many reasonable conclusions regarding what this finding indicates, and I have outlined two of the most likely here:

1. Many students were not able to estimate the values of each of the two fractions as being close to, but less than, 1.

2. Many students ignored the directions to estimate and actually found a common denominator, added $\frac{96}{104}$ plus $\frac{91}{104}$ and arrived at the answer of $\frac{187}{104}$, but then had no way to reason about the magnitude of $\frac{187}{104}$.

In the introduction to the CCSSM, the authors write that the standards represent a mix of procedural fluency and conceptual understanding because "[s]tudents who lack understanding of a topic may rely on procedures too heavily" (NGA Center/CCSSO 2010, 8). In the tenth edition of his book *Error Patterns in Computation: Using Error Patterns to Help Each Student Learn*, Robert B. Ashlock (2010) identifies several common errors that students make when attempting to add fractions, many of which represent misapplications or overgeneralizations of rules and procedures. For example, students may add across numerators and denominators (it works with fraction multiplication, so why not addition?), find common denominators without changing numerators, and/or disregard either the fractional part or whole number part of mixed numbers.

Petit, Laird, and Marsden (2010) state that, "[f]raction addition (and subtraction) concepts build from, and are dependent upon, foundational part-to-whole, equivalence, and magnitude ideas" (145). They stress repeatedly the importance of students' conceptual understanding as a means of estimating and reasoning about the results of addition, and share many examples of student work to illustrate this point. The authors make a strong case for their claim that procedural fluency and conceptual understanding work together, "each contributing to a deeper understanding of the other."

3.1   *Addition with Cuisenaire Rods, Version 1*

Overview

In this activity, students use Cuisenaire rods to understand addition as the joining of parts of the same-size whole. For all the problems in this activity, the brown rod is used as the whole.

1. Explain to students that they will be solving addition problems using Cuisenaire rods. Remind students of the work they have done previously to determine how to name fractional parts of wholes.

2. If students have not had much experience with Cuisenaire rods, you may want to give them a few minutes to explore the relationships among the rods.

3. Display the following problem for all students to see:

   $\frac{1}{2}$ of a brown rod + $\frac{1}{2}$ of a brown rod =

   _____ brown rod(s)

4. Students should have no trouble stating that the answer is 1 (or one whole) brown rod. Acknowledge that this is correct, but then ask how they could use the rods to prove to someone else that the answer is one brown rod.

Materials

Addition with Cuisenaire Rods, Version 1, recording sheets (**Reproducible 3a**), 1 per student

Cuisenaire rods, 1 set per pair of students

Manipulative Note

Cuisenaire rods are wooden or plastic blocks that range in length from 1 to 10 cm. Each rod of a given length is the same color. That is, all the 1-cm rods are white, all the 2-cm rods are red, all the 3-cm rods are light green, and so on.

This illustrates Strategy #10 of the ten essential strategies for supporting fraction sense: *Provide opportunities for students to build on their reasoning and sense-making skills about fractions by working with a variety of manipulatives and tools, such as Cuisenaire rods, Pattern Blocks, Fraction Kits, and ordinary items from their lives.* To learn more about this strategy, see Chapter 1 of *Beyond Pizzas & Pies: 10 Essential Strategies for Supporting Fraction Sense, Grades 3–5, Second Edition* (McNamara and Shaughnessy 2015).

This activity is a good follow-up to Activity 1.2, *Part to Whole and Whole to Part* **and Activity 3.1,** *Measuring with Cuisenaire Rods* **from Beyond Pizzas &** *Pies, Second Edition* **(McNamara and Shaughnessy, 2015).**

Classroom Activities

5. Encourage students to use what they know about fractional relationships to find two of the rods that are half as long as the brown rod, lay them end to end, and show that they are, in fact, the same length as one whole brown rod, as shown here:

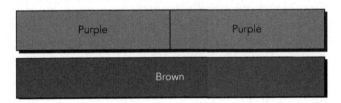

6. After students come to a consensus that the rods prove that $\frac{1}{2}$ brown rod plus $\frac{1}{2}$ brown rod does indeed equal 1 whole brown rod, display the following problem for all students to see:

$\frac{1}{4}$ brown rod + $\frac{1}{4}$ brown rod = _____ brown rod(s)

7. Students are again likely to answer that $\frac{1}{4}$ brown rod plus $\frac{1}{4}$ brown rod equals $\frac{1}{2}$ (or $\frac{2}{4}$) of a brown rod. Again, ask how they could use the rods to prove this answer is correct. They first need to determine which rod is the same length as $\frac{1}{4}$ of the brown rod and determine how long they are when placed end to end. Students may be content to answer that two of the red rods are the same length as the purple rod, which they already know is $\frac{1}{2}$ of the brown rod. Press them to explain again how they know the purple rod is $\frac{1}{2}$ the length of the brown rod.

This illustrates Strategy #3 of the ten essential strategies for supporting fraction sense: *Provide opportunities for students to recognize equivalent fractions as different ways to name the same quantity.* To learn more about this strategy, see Chapter 1 of *Beyond Pizzas & Pies: 10 Essential Strategies for Supporting Fraction Sense, Grades 3–5, Second Edition* (McNamara and Shaughnessy 2015).

Teaching Tip

It can be tempting to create a chart identifying the fractional relationships among the rods before beginning this activity. However, it is more beneficial for students to use the definition of a fraction to determine these relationships in the context of solving problems such as the ones included here.

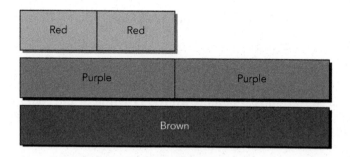

8. Next, display the following problem for all students to see:

$\frac{1}{2}$ brown rod + $\frac{1}{4}$ brown rod = _____ brown rod(s)

9. Students who are able to answer quickly, "Three-fourths of a brown rod," should be encouraged to use the Cuisenaire rods to prove their answer. For students who aren't sure how to proceed, suggest they think about how the first two problems were solved. Suggest that because they already know which rods to use (the purple and the red) they now need to determine what to call the combined length of the two rods.

10. If no one suggests it, ask how using equivalent fractions could help add $\frac{1}{2}$ and $\frac{1}{4}$. Ask if either fraction could be renamed so the two fractions have the same denominator.

11. Guide students to see that the purple rod is also the same length as two red rods, and because the red rods are $\frac{1}{4}$ of the brown rod, the problem could be solved by renaming $\frac{1}{2}$ to $\frac{2}{4}$ and adding $\frac{2}{4}$ to $\frac{1}{4}$, thus equaling $\frac{3}{4}$. The rods can then be used to prove the length of the rod equaling $\frac{1}{2}$ of the brown rod (the purple rod) and the rod equaling $\frac{1}{4}$ of the brown rod (the red rod) is the same as the length of three red rods, or $\frac{3}{4}$ of the brown rod.

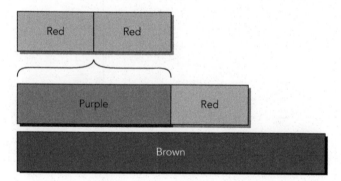

12. Display the following problem for all students to see:

$\frac{1}{4}$ brown rod + $\frac{7}{8}$ brown rod = _____ brown rod(s)

13. Students will likely determine the sum is greater than the length of 1 brown rod. If they don't, encourage them to compare the length of $\frac{1}{4}$ of a brown rod (1 red rod) plus $\frac{7}{8}$ of a brown rod (7 white or tan rods) with a brown rod as shown here. Students should see that the sum of $\frac{1}{4}$ of a brown rod and $\frac{7}{8}$ of a brown rod is $1\frac{1}{8}$ brown rods or $\frac{9}{8}$ brown rods.

14. Pass out the *Addition with Cuisenaire Rods*, Version 1, recording sheet and have students work in pairs or independently to solve the problems. (See Figure 3–1; also available as Reproducible 3a.) Monitor as students complete the problems and take note of which problems are especially challenging. When students have completed the sheet, have a few of them share their strategies for solving the problems that seemed to engender the most discussion and problem solving.

REPRODUCIBLE 3A

Addition with Cuisenaire Rods, Version 1, Recording Sheet

Date: _____

Name: _____

Directions: Use the Cuisenaire rods to solve the following problems.

1. $\frac{2}{4}$ brown rod + $\frac{1}{4}$ brown rod = _____ brown rod(s).

2. $\frac{1}{8}$ brown rod + $\frac{5}{8}$ brown rod = _____ brown rod(s).

3. $\frac{3}{4}$ brown rod + $\frac{6}{8}$ brown rod = _____ brown rod(s).

4. $1\frac{1}{4}$ brown rods + $\frac{1}{4}$ brown rod = _____ brown rod(s).

5. $\frac{3}{7}$ brown rod + $2\frac{4}{8}$ brown rods = _____ brown rod(s).

6. $2\frac{1}{4}$ brown rods + $3\frac{3}{4}$ brown rods = _____ brown rod(s).

7. $1\frac{1}{4}$ brown rods + $2\frac{5}{8}$ brown rods = _____ brown rod(s).

8. $3\frac{5}{8}$ brown rods + $2\frac{3}{4}$ brown rods = _____ brown rod(s).

Figure 3–1. *Addition with Cuisenaire Rods, Version 1, recording sheet*

3.2 Addition with Cuisenaire Rods, Version 2

Overview

As in Version 1, students use Cuisenaire rods to add fractions with unlike denominators. Unlike Version 1, the whole changes in each problem, thus helping students learn that fractions such as $\frac{1}{2}$ and $\frac{4}{5}$ are not names for specific rods, but rather descriptions of relationships between the rod designated as the part and the rod length designated as the whole.

1. If students have completed *Addition with Cuisenaire Rods*, Version 1, tell them that *Addition with Cuisenaire Rods*, Version 2, involves similar problems, but instead of always using the brown rod as the whole, each problem uses a different rod.

2. You may want to have students work independently or with a partner to solve the first problem, then process their responses with the whole class. Many students are likely to assume that in Problem 1 they can use the red rod to represent $\frac{1}{4}$ because the red rod was used as $\frac{1}{4}$ of the brown rod. This is a perfect time to revisit and reinforce what it means for something to be $\frac{1}{4}$ (or $\frac{1}{2}$ or $\frac{1}{8}$ or $\frac{1}{n}$) of something else. When students seem sure of the process, pass out the *Addition with Cuisenaire Rods*, Version 2, recording sheets. (See Figure 3–2; also available as Reproducible 3b.)

Materials

Addition with Cuisenaire Rods, Version 2, recording sheets (**Reproducible 3b**), 1 per student

Cuisenaire rods, 1 set per pair of students

This illustrates Strategy #4 of the ten essential strategies for supporting fraction sense: *Provide opportunities for students to work with changing units.* To learn more about this strategy, see Chapter 1 of *Beyond Pizzas & Pies: 10 Essential Strategies for Supporting Fraction Sense, Grades 3–5, Second Edition* (McNamara and Shaughnessy 2015).

REPRODUCIBLE 3B

Addition with Cuisenaire Rods, Version 2, Recording Sheet

Directions: Use the Cuisenaire rods to solve the following problems.

1. $\frac{1}{8}$ orange rod + $\frac{1}{4}$ orange rod = _____ orange rod(s).

2. $\frac{3}{4}$ purple rod + $\frac{1}{2}$ purple rod = _____ purple rod(s).

3. $\frac{2}{3}$ dark green rod + $\frac{1}{6}$ dark green rod = _____ dark green rod(s).

4. $1\frac{1}{2}$ red rods + $1\frac{1}{2}$ red rods = _____ red rod(s).

5. $2\frac{1}{2}$ orange rods + $2\frac{4}{5}$ orange rods = _____ orange rod(s).

6. $2\frac{2}{3}$ dark green rods + $1\frac{1}{2}$ dark green rods = _____ dark green rod(s).

7. $1\frac{3}{5}$ orange rods + $2\frac{1}{2}$ orange rods = _____ orange rod(s).

8. $1\frac{1}{2}$ dark green rods + $3\frac{1}{3}$ dark green rods = _____ dark green rod(s).

Figure 3–2. *Addition with Cuisenaire Rods, Version 2, recording sheet*

3.3   Make a One

Overview

This activity (adapted from Burns [2003]) gives students a problem-solving experience that also provides practice with combining fractions in multiple ways. Students first solve a problem with unlimited solutions: finding five fractions that add to 1. They then revisit the problem, this time with the limitation of using cards they draw from a deck with ten each of 1s, 2s, 4s, and 8s to form the fractions. For a second version of the activity, students use a deck with ten cards each of 1s, 3s, 6s, and 12s; for a third version, they use both decks.

Materials

Make a One, recording sheets (**Reproducible 3c**), 1 per pair of students

Make a One, Version 1, cards, (**Reproducible 3d** copied on one color of card stock), 1 set per group of 4 students

Make a One, Version 2, cards, (**Reproducible 3e** copied on a different color of card stock), 1 set per group of 4 students

Make a One, rules (**Reproducible 3f**), 1 per group of 4 students, optional

---

1. Display the *Make a One* recording sheet and challenge students to think of five fractions that add up to 1. (See Figure 3–3; also available as Reproducible 3c.) Allow time for students to think on their own first, and then discuss their ideas with a partner. A set of boxes looks like this:

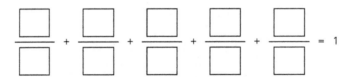

2. Ask for a volunteer to present a solution. Record it and ask the volunteer to explain why the fractions add up to 1. Encourage him or her to refer to any materials or representations that students have used to develop their understanding of fractions.

3. Display another set of boxes and repeat with another volunteer. Continue until you have recorded five solutions.

4. Introduce the scoring system for the activity. Show students the *Make a One* recording sheet and point out that there are spaces for five solutions, just as you recorded when introducing the activity, and that next to each equation is a line for the score for that round. Explain as follows: "You score one point for each number you write in the numerator or denominator. Each of the five solutions we've come up with so far used ten numbers, so each round would score ten points. The total score for these five rounds is fifty points."

5. Introduce the deck of cards for Version 1, and relate that it contains forty cards, ten each of 1s, 2s, 4s, and 8s. (See Figure 3–4; also available as Reproducible 3d.) Explain the rules, either displaying them or distributing them to students as you do so. (See Figure 3–5; also available as Reproducible 3f.)

6. Tell students that with this limited set of numbers, it's difficult to use all ten of the cards they draw to make five fractions that add to 1. Explain that they may only be able to make four fractions, or three or two or one, but their goal is to use as many of their cards as they can during each round to get as high a score as possible. You may want to model an example by drawing ten cards and having students work with a partner to use as many of the numbers as possible to make fractions that add to 1.

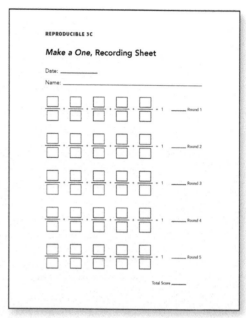

Figure 3–3. *Make a One,* recording sheet

7. Have students play in teams of two against other teams of two to increase their opportunities to discuss their strategies and share their thinking. As students play, circulate and offer help

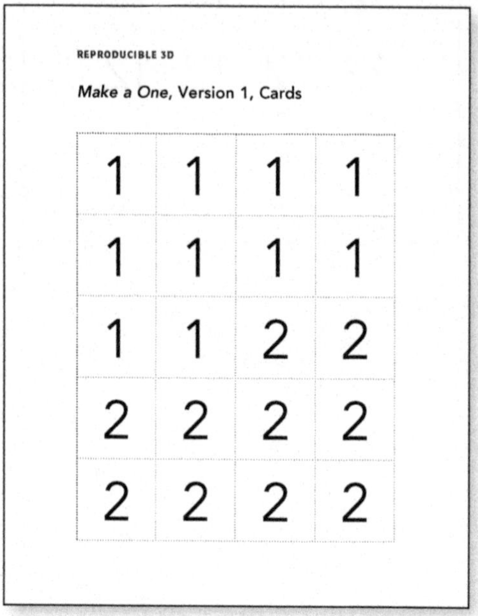

Figure 3–4. *Make a One,* Version 1, cards

REPRODUCIBLE 3F

Make a One, Rules

You need:

- One deck of forty cards, ten each of 1s, 2s, 4s, and 8s (for Version 1)
- One deck of forty cards, ten each of 1s, 3s, 6s, and 12s (for Version 2)
- One *Make a One* Recording Sheet
- A partner and another pair to play with

Rules for Version 1

1. One person mixes the Version 1 deck of cards and leaves them facedown.
2. Each pair takes ten cards.
3. Use as many of your cards as you can to make fractions that add to 1. Write the fractions on your recording sheet and fill in your score. You score 1 point for each box you fill in when making your fractions.
4. When everyone has completed the round, return to Step 1 and continue.
5. Play five rounds and figure your total score. The team with the highest score wins.

Rules for Version 2

Play the same way as you do for Version 1, but use the Version 2 deck of cards.

Rules for Version 3

Play the same way as you do for Versions 1 and 2, but shuffle both decks of cards together and use all the cards.

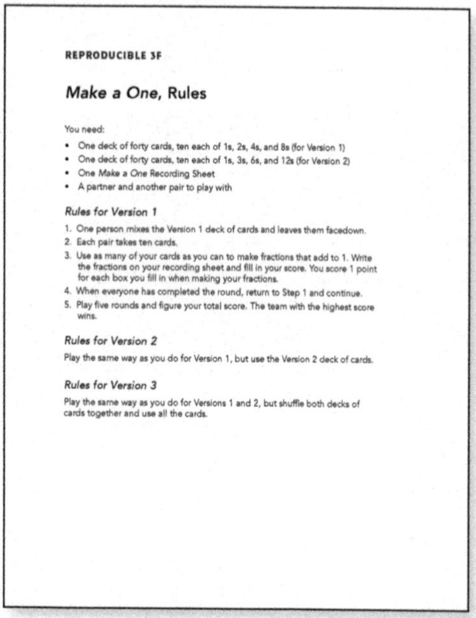

Figure 3–5. *Make a One,* rules

as needed. Make sure you have plenty of recording sheets available so students who finish quickly can play again.

8. After students have had ample time to play Version 1, introduce the second deck of cards and have students play again. (See Figure 3–6; also available as Reproducible 3e.)

9. Introduce a third version of the activity by having students shuffle the two decks together.

10. After everyone has played at least Version 1 and Version 2, bring the students back together and discuss the strategies that helped them use as many of their cards as possible.

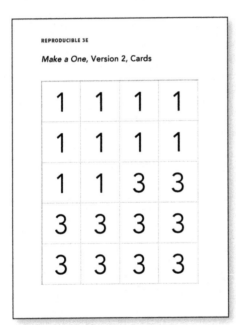
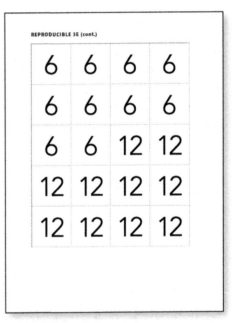

Figure 3–6. *Make a One*, Version 2, cards

3.4 Get to the Whole, Version 1

Materials
Get to the Whole, Version 1, recording sheets (**Reproducible 3g**), 1 per pair of students

Overview

In this activity, students use their knowledge of equivalent fractions to decompose and recompose addends to "get to the whole." In Version 1, students add fractions with like denominators, starting with sums between 1 and 2, then moving on to adding fractions and mixed numbers to sums greater than 2. Students are encouraged to use the commutative and associative properties to enable getting to the next whole number more easily.

1. Remind students of previous work they have done decomposing whole numbers when they add. You may want to ask if anyone uses the "Make a 10" strategy when adding two numbers such as 8 and 5. (To use the "Make a 10" strategy, to add 8 + 5, one decomposes 5 into 2 + 3, then adds 2 to 8 to get 10, then adds 3 to get 13.)

....

VIDEO CLIP 3a

Reviewing the "Make a 10" Strategy

In this clip, we see Ms. Kretschmar introducing Activity 3.4 by reminding students of the "Make a 10" strategy they used when playing "Oh No, 99!" How does reminding students of a successful strategy for whole number addition prepare them for success with fraction addition?

To view this video clip, scan the QR code or access via http://hein.pub/MathOLR

For commentary on the above, see the Appendix: Author's Video Reflections.

....

2. Tell students that, today, they will be adding fractions and, instead of decomposing one of the addends to make a 10, they will be decomposing one of the addends to make a 1 or the next whole number—in other words, to get to the whole.

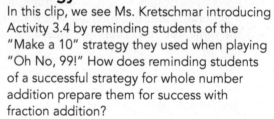

This illustrates Strategy #8 of the ten essential strategies for supporting fraction sense: *Provide students with multiple strategies for comparing and reasoning about fractions.* To learn more about this strategy, see Chapter I of *Beyond Pizzas & Pies: 10 Essential Strategies for Supporting Fraction Sense, Grades 3–5, Second Edition* (McNamara and Shaughnessy 2015).

Introducing "Get to the Whole"

After reviewing the "Make a 10" strategy for working with whole numbers, Ms. Kretschmar introduces "Get to the Whole." Why does Ms. Kretschmar select the fractions $\frac{3}{4}$ and $\frac{2}{5}$?

To view this video clip, scan the QR code or access via http://hein.pub/MathOLR

For commentary on the above, see the Appendix: Author's Video Reflections.

3. Display the fraction $\frac{3}{4}$. Ask students whether $\frac{3}{4}$ is equal to 1 whole. Then ask, "How many fourths do you need to equal one whole?" (This is a good opportunity to review the fraction equivalents to 1 and to establish a generalizable rule such as: When the numerator and denominator are the same, the fraction is equivalent to 1.)

4. Display the problem $\frac{3}{4} + \frac{3}{4}$ for all students to see. Ask if there is any way to decompose one of the addends to get to the whole. If necessary, remind students that $\frac{3}{4}$ is made up of three $\frac{1}{4}$s, or $\frac{1}{4}$ plus $\frac{1}{4}$ plus $\frac{1}{4}$. Suggest that one of the $\frac{1}{4}$s could be added to $\frac{3}{4}$ to get to the whole, leaving two more $\frac{1}{4}$s. The resulting sum is $1\frac{2}{4}$ or $1\frac{1}{2}$.

$$\frac{3}{4} + \frac{3}{4}$$

$$\frac{3}{4} + \frac{1}{4} + \frac{1}{4} + \frac{1}{4}$$

$$\left(\frac{3}{4} + \frac{1}{4}\right) + \frac{1}{4} + \frac{1}{4}$$

$$1 + \frac{2}{4}$$

Using the Properties of Operations

Students use the commutative and associative properties intuitively as they decompose, reorder, and regroup fractions to add them.

5. Another strategy you may see is to decompose both $\frac{3}{4}$ into $\frac{1}{2}$ plus $\frac{1}{4}$, then group the halves and the fourths: $\left(\frac{1}{2} + \frac{1}{2}\right) + \left(\frac{1}{4} + \frac{1}{4}\right)$.

VIDEO CLIP 3c

$\frac{3}{4} + \frac{3}{4}$: Will's Strategy

In this clip, we see Will sharing his strategy for decomposing and recomposing $\frac{3}{4} + \frac{3}{4}$. What is Will's strategy? What mathematical properties does Will use in his strategy? What does Ms. Kretschmar do to help other students understand Will's thinking?

To view this video clip, scan the QR code or access via http://hein.pub/MathOLR

For commentary on the above, see the Appendix: Author's Video Reflections.

VIDEO CLIP 3d

$\frac{3}{4} + \frac{3}{4}$: Belen's Strategy

In this clip, Ms. Kretschmar presses Belen to describe another strategy for decomposing and recomposing $\frac{3}{4} + \frac{3}{4}$. What is Belen's strategy, and how might students' previous use of the Cuisenaire rods have encouraged Belen's strategy?

To view this video clip, scan the QR code or access via http://hein.pub/MathOLR

For commentary on the above, see the Appendix: Author's Video Reflections.

6. Repeat the process with the problem $\frac{3}{5} + \frac{4}{5}$. Ask students to talk with a partner and decide whether they can decompose one of the addends to get to the whole. Students may not realize that either addend can be decomposed—and that just as with whole number addition, the order in which the two numbers are added does not matter. An example from whole number addition may, again, be helpful for students. When adding two numbers such as 2 and 18, it's more efficient to start with the 18 and then add the 2, than to start with the 2 and then add the 18.

VIDEO CLIP 3e

$\frac{3}{5} + \frac{4}{5}$: Malaya's Strategy

After students have discussed their strategies with a partner, we hear Malaya describe her strategy for adding $\frac{3}{5} + \frac{4}{5}$. What is Malaya's strategy, and how does Ms. Kretschmar help other students understand Malaya's thinking?

To view this video clip, scan the QR code or access via http://hein.pub/MathOLR

For commentary on the above, see the Appendix: Author's Video Reflections.

VIDEO CLIP 3f

$\frac{3}{5} + \frac{4}{5}$: Yuli's Use of Academic Language

After hearing from Malaya, Ms. Kretschmar asks Yuli to share her strategy for adding $\frac{3}{5}$ and $\frac{4}{5}$. How does explaining her strategy to her classmates encourage Yuli's use of academic language?

To view this video clip, scan the QR code or access via http://hein.pub/MathOLR

For commentary on the above, see the Appendix: Author's Video Reflections.

---

7. Continue with problems such as $\frac{5}{9} + \frac{8}{9}$, $\frac{3}{8} + \frac{7}{8}$, $\frac{4}{6} + \frac{3}{6}$, and so on.

8. When students are comfortable using the "Get to the Whole" strategy with proper fractions, introduce the following problems involving sums greater than 2: $1\frac{2}{3} + \frac{2}{3}$, $4\frac{3}{10} + \frac{9}{10}$, $\frac{8}{9} + 2\frac{4}{9}$.

   Strategies that students use may include the following:

   $1\frac{2}{3} + \frac{2}{3}$: Decomposing the second $\frac{2}{3}$ into $\frac{1}{3}$ plus $\frac{1}{3}$, then adding $(1\frac{2}{3} + \frac{1}{3}) + \frac{1}{3}$

   $4\frac{3}{10} + \frac{9}{10}$: Decomposing $\frac{9}{10}$ into $\frac{7}{10}$ and $\frac{2}{10}$, then adding $(4\frac{3}{10} + \frac{7}{10}) + \frac{2}{10}$; decomposing $4\frac{3}{10}$ into 4 plus $\frac{3}{10}$, decomposing $\frac{3}{10}$ into $\frac{1}{10}$ and $\frac{2}{10}$, then adding $4 + (\frac{1}{10} + \frac{9}{10}) + \frac{2}{10}$

   $\frac{8}{9} + 2\frac{4}{9}$: Decomposing $2\frac{4}{9}$ into 2 plus $\frac{1}{9}$ plus $\frac{3}{9}$, then adding $(\frac{8}{9} + \frac{1}{9}) + 2 + \frac{3}{9}$; decomposing $\frac{8}{9}$ into $\frac{5}{9}$ plus $\frac{3}{9}$, then adding $2 + (\frac{4}{9} + \frac{5}{9}) + \frac{3}{9}$

9. For more practice with the "Get to the Whole" strategy, pass out the *Get to the Whole*, Version 1, recording sheet. (See Figure 3–7; also available as Reproducible 3g.)

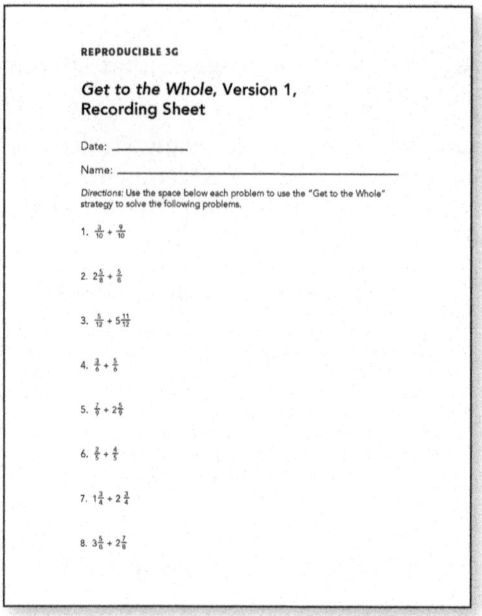

REPRODUCIBLE 3G

***Get to the Whole*, Version 1, Recording Sheet**

Date: ________

Name: ________________

Directions: Use the space below each problem to use the "Get to the Whole" strategy to solve the following problems.

1. $\frac{3}{10} + \frac{9}{10}$
2. $2\frac{5}{8} + \frac{5}{8}$
3. $\frac{5}{12} + 5\frac{11}{12}$
4. $\frac{3}{6} + \frac{5}{6}$
5. $\frac{7}{9} + 2\frac{5}{9}$
6. $\frac{2}{5} + \frac{4}{5}$
7. $1\frac{3}{4} + 2\frac{3}{4}$
8. $3\frac{5}{8} + 2\frac{7}{8}$

Figure 3–7. *Get to the Whole*, Version 1, recording sheet

Get to the Whole, Version 2

Materials
Get to the Whole, Version 2, recording sheets (**Reproducible 3h**), 1 per pair of students

Overview

In *Get to the Whole*, Version 2, students add fractions and mixed numbers with unlike denominators. As in Version 1, students are encouraged to use the commutative and associative properties to enable getting to the next whole number more easily.

1. Remind students of previous work they have done decomposing fractions when they add.

2. Tell them that, today, they will be adding fractions and mixed numbers like before (*Get to the Whole*, Version 1), but the fractions will have different denominators.

3. Display the problem $\frac{1}{2} + \frac{3}{4}$ for all students to see. Ask, "Is there any way to decompose one of the addends to get to the whole?" If necessary, ask students, "Is there an equivalent to $\frac{1}{2}$ or $\frac{3}{4}$ that you could use to get to the whole?"

4. If no one has an idea to share, suggest that students talk to a partner about the problem.

5. After a few minutes of partner talk, bring students back together to discuss how to decompose one of the addends. Record students' responses, making sure to ask students to explain. Two strategies students are likely to use are shown here:

Strategy 1: Decompose $\frac{3}{4}$

$$\frac{1}{2} + \frac{3}{4}$$

$$\frac{1}{2} + \frac{2}{4} + \frac{1}{4}$$

$$\left(\frac{1}{2} + \frac{2}{4}\right) + \frac{1}{4}$$

$$1 + \frac{1}{4}$$

Strategy 2: Decompose $\frac{1}{2}$

$$\frac{1}{2} + \frac{3}{4}$$

$$\frac{1}{4} + \frac{1}{4} + \frac{3}{4}$$

$$\frac{1}{4} + \left(\frac{1}{4} + \frac{3}{4}\right)$$

$$\frac{1}{4} + 1$$

6. Repeat the process with the problem $1\frac{5}{6} + \frac{2}{3}$. Ask students to talk with a partner and decide how they can decompose one of the addends to get to the whole.

7. Continue with problems such as $2\frac{1}{3} + \frac{11}{12}$, $3\frac{1}{2} + \frac{9}{10}$, $1\frac{5}{8} + \frac{3}{4}$, and so on.

Strategies that students use may include:

$2\frac{1}{3} + \frac{11}{12}$: Decomposing $2\frac{1}{3}$ into 2 plus $\frac{1}{3}$, and then renaming $\frac{1}{3}$ as $\frac{4}{12}$ and decomposing $\frac{4}{12}$ into $\frac{3}{12}$ plus $\frac{1}{12}$, then adding $2 + \frac{3}{12} + (\frac{1}{12} + \frac{11}{12})$

$3\frac{1}{2} + \frac{9}{10}$: Decomposing $\frac{9}{10}$ into $\frac{5}{10}$ plus $\frac{4}{10}$, renaming $\frac{5}{10}$ as $\frac{1}{2}$, then adding $(3\frac{1}{2} + \frac{1}{2}) + \frac{4}{10}$

$1\frac{5}{8} + \frac{3}{4}$: Renaming $\frac{3}{4}$ as $\frac{6}{8}$, decomposing $\frac{6}{8}$ into $\frac{3}{8}$ plus $\frac{3}{8}$, then adding $(1\frac{5}{8} + \frac{3}{8}) + \frac{3}{8}$

8. For more practice with the "Get to the Whole" strategy, pass out the *Get to the Whole*, Version 2, recording sheet. (See Figure 3–8; also available as Reproducible 3h.)

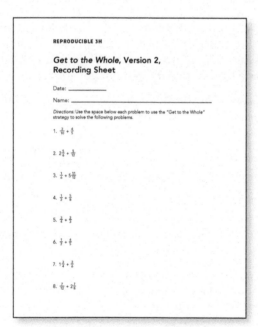

Figure 3–8. *Get to the Whole*, Version 2, recording sheet

Tell Me All You Can, Addition

Materials
none

Overview

This routine (adapted from Bresser and Holzman [2006]) can be used in any content area and is especially helpful when addressing content or concepts that may look somewhat new to students. Students are shown a problem such as $4\frac{5}{6} + 1\frac{3}{8}$ and are told to look closely at the numbers and operations involved. Before coming up with an exact answer, have students consider and discuss everything they know about the problem as a means of getting a sense of the "neighborhood" of the answer. Problems can be chosen to highlight specific strategies such as estimation and the use of benchmarks, and to bring to light common challenges and misconceptions students often have.

This illustrates Strategy #9 of the ten essential strategies for supporting fraction sense: *Provide opportunities for students to engage in mathematical discourse and share and discuss their mathematical ideas, even those that may not be fully formed or completely accurate.* To learn more about this strategy, see Chapter 1 of *Beyond Pizzas & Pies: 10 Essential Strategies for Supporting Fraction Sense, Grades 3–5, Second Edition* (McNamara and Shaughnessy 2015).

1. Begin by displaying the problem $\frac{1}{2} + \frac{1}{4}$, and tell students you don't want them to give you an exact answer, but instead to tell you all they can about the answer. If students have trouble coming up with ideas, the following sentence frames may help them get started:

   - The answer will be more than _____ because _____.
     (*The answer will be more than $\frac{1}{2}$ because we're starting with $\frac{1}{2}$ and adding more to it.*)

   - The answer will be less than _____ because _____.
     (*The answer will be less than 1 because $\frac{1}{2} + \frac{1}{2} = 1$, and $\frac{1}{4}$ is less than $\frac{1}{2}$.*)

   - The answer will be between _____ and _____ because _____.

     (*The answer will be between $\frac{1}{2}$ and 1, because we're adding to $\frac{1}{2}$, but not enough to get to 1.*)

2. You may also ask students questions such as, "Will the answer be more or less than one-half? How do you know?" and "Will the answer be more or less than one? How do you know?"

3. Tell students to turn and talk to their neighbor or elbow partner and share their ideas about the answer.

4. When students have had adequate time to discuss the problem with their partner, ask for volunteers to share an idea (either one they thought of or one they heard from their partner) with the whole class.

5. Chart students' contributions and be sure to ask students for their rationale if they do not provide it without prompting.

6. Display another problem and repeat the process.

7. Suggestions for addressing different problem types are as follows:

Adding fractions with like denominators

$\frac{2}{3} + \frac{2}{3}$: The answer will be more than one because two-thirds plus one third equals one, and we're adding another one-third. The answer will be less than two because we need six-thirds to make two and we only have four-thirds.

Adding fractions with unlike denominators

$\frac{1}{2} + \frac{2}{3}$: The answer will be more than 1 because $\frac{1}{2} + \frac{1}{2} = 1$, and $\frac{2}{3}$ is more than 1/2.

$\frac{3}{4} + \frac{1}{6}$: The answer will be less than 1 because $\frac{3}{4} + \frac{1}{4} = 1$, and $\frac{1}{6}$ is less than $\frac{1}{4}$.

Adding mixed numbers

$4\frac{5}{6} + 1\frac{1}{12}$: The answer will be more than 5 because the whole numbers alone (4 and 1) add up to 5. The answer will be less than 6 because $\frac{5}{6} + \frac{1}{6} = 1$, and $\frac{1}{12}$ is less than $\frac{1}{6}$.

The understanding that fractions are numbers that can be added using strategies such as decomposition and recomposition, as well as properties of operations, is an essential aspect of understanding fractions. As students use this knowledge to add fractions, they are deepening their conceptual understanding and developing strategies for fraction addition that are flexible and responsive to the numbers involved. In addition, by using their knowledge of equivalent fractions to add fractions with unlike denominators, students strengthen and use their understanding that equivalent fractions are different ways of naming the same number. In this way, students' strategies for fraction addition "build on previous understandings," as called for in the Common Core State Standards for Mathematics.

Study Questions

After Reading Chapter 3

1. What information presented in the "Classroom Scenario," "What's the Math?," and "What's the Research?" sections was familiar to you or similar to your experience with students?

2. Using their knowledge of equivalent fractions to add fractions with unlike denominators is a somewhat different approach to adding fractions than we have seen in the past. How will this change influence how you approach adding fractions with your students?

3. Which of the Classroom Activities (Activity 3.1: *Addition with Cuisenaire Rods*, Version 1; Activity 3.2: *Addition with Cuisenaire Rods*, Version 2; Activity 3.3: *Make a One*; Activity 3.4: *Get to the Whole*, Version 1; Activity 3.5: *Get to the Whole*, Version 2; Activity 3.6: *Tell Me All You Can*) do you plan to implement with your students?

After Trying One or More of the Activities

1. Describe the activity and any modifications you made to meet your students' needs or to align with your curriculum.

2. How did this activity add to your knowledge of what your students do and do not understand about adding fractions?

3. What are your next steps for supporting your students' learning about adding fractions?

Connections to *Beyond Pizzas & Pies, Second Edition*

Beyond Invert & Multiply builds on the foundational understandings introduced in its companion resource, *Beyond Pizzas & Pies: 10 Essential Strategies for Supporting Fraction Sense, Grades 3–5, Second Edition*. I recommend pairing this chapter with Chapters 3 and 4 in *Beyond Pizzas & Pies, Second Edition*, to continue your learning.

Making Sense

Subtraction with Fractions

OUTLINE

CCSS Connections

Prerequisite Standards

3.NF.A.1: Understand a fraction $1/b$ as the quantity formed by 1 part when a whole is partitioned into b equal parts; understand a fraction a/b as the quantity formed by a parts of size $1/b$.

3.NF.A.2: Understand a fraction as a number on the number line; represent fractions on a number line diagram.

Standards Addressed

4.NF.B.3: Understand a fraction a/b with $a > 1$ as a sum of fractions $1/b$.

4.NF.B.3a: Understand addition and subtraction of fractions as joining and separating parts referring to the same whole.

4.NF.B.3b: Decompose a fraction into a sum of fractions with the same denominator in more than one way, recording each decomposition by an equation. Justify decompositions, e.g., by using a visual fraction model.

4.NF.B.3c: Add and subtract mixed numbers with like denominators, e.g., by replacing each mixed number with an equivalent fraction, and/or by using properties of operations and the relationship between addition and subtraction.

5.NF.A.1: Add and subtract fractions with unlike denominators (including mixed numbers) by replacing given fractions with equivalent fractions in such a way as to produce an equivalent sum or difference of fractions with like denominators.

As Mrs. Ahmed headed into the library for the monthly meeting with her fourth-grade colleagues, she glanced down at Naomi's paper once again. She thought her students had a pretty solid understanding of fractions in general and were well on their way to being able to subtract proper fractions and mixed numbers as long as they had like denominators. Naomi was generally one of the students she could count on to grasp concepts quickly and, often, to explain ideas during class discussions in ways that benefitted the rest of the students. For this reason, Mrs. Ahmed was completely puzzled by Naomi's responses on her end-of-class check. Of the eight problems on the page, Naomi had answered only two correctly, $3\frac{3}{10} - 1\frac{7}{10}$ and $5\frac{1}{10} - 4\frac{9}{10}$. The other problems were very similar in that they involved subtracting mixed numbers with regrouping, with the exception that they had denominators other than 10.

End of Class Check

1. $3\frac{3}{10}$

   $-1\frac{7}{10}$

   _____

2. $5\frac{3}{8}$

   $-4\frac{7}{8}$

   _____

3. $4\frac{1}{4}$

   $-3\frac{3}{4}$

   _____

4. $2\frac{1}{6}$

   $-\frac{5}{6}$

   _____

5. $5\frac{1}{10}$

   $-4\frac{9}{10}$

   _____

6. $4\frac{1}{12}$

   $-1\frac{7}{12}$

   _____

While Mrs. Ahmed waited for her colleagues to join her, she realized she had been so intrigued by Naomi's responses that she hadn't looked at the rest of the papers in her hand. As she went through the pile, she noticed that a handful of other students had very similar responses to Naomi. On the problems that had a denominator of 10, they were able to find the correct answer; but, on problems with other denominators, their answers were wrong. Mrs. Ahmed was glad she was meeting with her colleagues today so they could help her figure out what the students were doing.

After the initial check-in Mrs. Ahmed asked if she could share something that was puzzling her. She passed out the students' papers that showed the same pattern as Naomi and was a bit relieved to see that her colleagues were also puzzled by the students' responses. As they often did, the teachers first began talking about what the students seemed to know, based on their answers on the papers. The teachers agreed that Naomi and her classmates understood the need for regrouping in the problems on the end-of-class check, but seemed confused about what to regroup.

"They are fine when the denominator is ten," Ms. Alvarez began, "but I don't know what they're doing on the other problems."

"I know," responded Mrs. Ahmed. "That's what I see, too, but I am really baffled by what they are doing on the problems with the other fractions."

"Wait a minute, wait a minute, I think I figured it out!" Ms. Lee said as she got up and went to the whiteboard.

"On problems with ten in the denominator, like this," Ms. Lee noted, as she wrote $3\frac{3}{10} - 1\frac{7}{10}$ on the board, "they cross out the three and make it a two and make the numerator of the minuend thirteen. Then, they subtract seven-tenths from thirteen-tenths to get six-tenths, then subtract the whole numbers to get one and six-tenths. This works just fine *as long as* the denominators are tenths."

The other teachers nodded in agreement at Ms. Lee's modeling of the students' strategy.

"But," Ms. Lee continued, "when the denominators are not tenths, they are doing the same thing and still regrouping ten. So, in problem two," she said, as she wrote $5\frac{3}{8} - 4\frac{7}{8}$, on the board, "when they regroup, they end up with four and thirteen-eighths minus four and seven-eighths instead of four and eleven-eighths minus four and seven-eighths."

"Wait. I'm not following you," remarked Mr. Collins, who had just moved up to teach fourth graders instead of kindergarteners and had never taught fractions before. "Can you go over that again?"

"Let me try," Mrs. Ahmed requested, "so that I know how to address this in class tomorrow."

As Mrs. Ahmed used Naomi's strategy to solve $4\frac{1}{4} - 3\frac{3}{4}$, Mr. Collins acknowledged that he understood what she was doing. "I think that's what they call a 'buggy' algorithm," he said. "I remember reading about those in my credential program. It's when kids misapply or overgeneralize procedures. I knew that students often added and subtracted across numerators and denominators, but I had no idea they did stuff like this with fractions. Boy have I got a lot to learn about teaching fourth grade!"

"Well, lucky for you, you have us to help you! Thanks, everybody. I feel much better prepared to address this tomorrow," Mrs. Ahmed said, the relief in her voice apparent. "Who else has something they'd like to bring to the group?"

n my work with classroom teachers, I often ask them to write a subtraction problem they might use with their students. Most of the problems people write are similar to "At the beginning of the year we had 28 students in our class. Three students moved away. How many students do we have now?" and fall into the category of *Separate—result unknown*. (See Chapter 2, Table 2–1, for more information on addition and subtraction problem types.) In the primary grades, these problems are often referred to as *take-away problems* and they make up the bulk of the subtraction problems that students encounter in their curricular materials. Students are taught to represent the starting quantity with materials, drawings, or tallies, and then to remove, cross out, or erase to show the "take-away." To develop a robust concept of subtraction, however, students must also be able to interpret other problem types, such as *Part–Part–Whole* and *Compare*, and to understand that subtraction can also mean the *difference* between two values, as in the following situation:

> Souleman and Jazmin planted seeds in science class. When they measured them after a week, Souleman's seed had grown into a 10-cm seedling and Jazmin's seed had grown into a 12-cm seedling. How much taller is Jazmin's seedling than Souleman's?

The two values in this scenario are 10 and 12, and one could surely arrive at the correct answer by subtracting 10 from 12. Given the context of the problem, however, approaching this situation as a take-away problem makes little sense, because what is being sought is the difference between the heights of the two plants, not what is left of the starting value when something is removed.

As with addition, students need opportunities to encounter subtraction situations of three problem types—*Separate*, *Part–Part–Whole*, and *Compare*—when dealing with fractions. Students need to reason about the numbers involved and make decisions about how best to solve a given problem. For example, a problem such as $5\frac{1}{3} - 4\frac{2}{3}$ could be solved by regrouping the $5\frac{1}{3}$ into $4\frac{4}{3}$. It can also be solved by counting up two $\frac{1}{3}$s from $4\frac{2}{3}$ to arrive at $5\frac{1}{3}$, as illustrated on the number line.

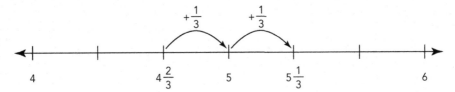

Understanding that not all subtraction situations represent a *Separate* context or must be solved using a take-away method is an essential aspect of understanding subtraction. This is no less true when students are working with fractions than when they are solving subtraction problems involving whole numbers.

N ot surprisingly, students' challenges with fraction subtraction are similar to those encountered with fraction addition (Siegler et al. 2010). Some of the most common difficulties students encounter are addressed briefly here:

- Students treat numerators and denominators as separate whole numbers and subtract across both (for example, $\frac{5}{6} - \frac{3}{4} = \frac{2}{2}$).
- When attempting to create fractions with common denominators, students fail to create equivalent fractions, and they change only the denominator of a fraction without making the corresponding change to the numerator (for example, given the problem $\frac{2}{3} - \frac{1}{6}$, students change it to $\frac{2}{6} - \frac{1}{6}$).
- Students ignore the fractional parts of mixed numbers and subtract only the whole numbers (for example, $6\frac{1}{4} - 4\frac{1}{2} = 2$).
- Students think that whole numbers have the same denominators as the fraction in a problem, so they attempt to change a problem such as $4 - \frac{3}{8}$ into $\frac{4}{8} - \frac{3}{8}$.

Among the strategies suggested to address and prevent such difficulties are the use of concrete objects and pictorial representations, the use of meaningful problems, the use of focused discussion around computational errors, and the use of estimation.

Although using realistic situations can be a very effective way of helping students understand computational problems, the use of contexts can also create surprising challenges. In looking at prospective teachers' understanding of fraction computation, Juli Dixon, a professor of mathematics education at the University of Central Florida in Orlando, and Jennifer Tobias, an assistant professor of mathematics education at Illinois State University in Normal, discuss the scenarios prospective teachers (their "students") wrote for the problem $\frac{3}{4} - \frac{1}{2}$ (Dixon and Tobias 2013). The authors identified the following situations their students might write for the problem:

1. Aubrey had $\frac{3}{4}$ of a pizza in a box. Before she began to eat, her dog ate $\frac{1}{2}$ of a pizza right out of the box. How much pizza did Aubrey have left after her dog ate some?

2. Darrell has $\frac{3}{4}$ of a cheese pizza leftover from his birthday. He eats $\frac{1}{2}$ of the leftover pizza. How much pizza does Darrell have left?

Both of the problem situations use the fractions $\frac{3}{4}$ and $\frac{1}{2}$, and both of them involve subtraction. Only the first situation, however, can be solved by subtracting $\frac{1}{2}$ from $\frac{3}{4}$, because the $\frac{3}{4}$ of the pizza in the box and the $\frac{1}{2}$ of a pizza eaten by the dog refer to the same whole (1 pizza). In the second situation, the whole is actually the $\frac{3}{4}$ of a pizza that Darrell has left over from his birthday.

The $\frac{1}{2}$ that he eats is $\frac{1}{2}$ of that $\frac{3}{4}$, or $\frac{3}{8}$ of the original pizza. What is left is the other $\frac{3}{8}$ of the original pizza. The calculation that corresponds to this situation is $\frac{3}{4} - (\frac{1}{2} \times \frac{3}{4})$.

Dixon and Tobias found that using situations like the one just described provided them with springboards for addressing their students' errors and deepening their understanding of what it means to operate with fractions. The following classroom activities are designed to provide similar opportunities for you to help your students explore subtraction with fractions, identify and discuss common errors and challenges, build on their understanding of subtraction with whole numbers, and deepen their understanding of fraction computation.

4.1 Subtraction with Cuisenaire Rods, Version 1

Classroom Activities

Overview

In this activity, students use Cuisenaire rods to understand subtraction as the separating of parts of the same-sized whole. For all the problems in this activity, the brown rod is used as the whole.

Materials

Subtraction with Cuisenaire Rods, Version 1, recording sheet (**Reproducible 4a**), 1 per student

Cuisenaire rods, 1 set per pair of students

1. Explain to students that they will be solving subtraction problems using Cuisenaire rods. Remind students of the work they have done previously to determine how to name fractional parts of wholes.

Manipulative Note

Cuisenaire rods are wooden or plastic blocks that range in length from 1 cm to 10 cm. Each rod of a given length is the same color. That is, all the 1-cm rods are white, all the 2-cm rods are red, all the 3-cm rods are light green, and so on.

2. If students have not had much experience with Cuisenaire rods, you may want to give them a few minutes to explore the relationships among the rods.

3. Display the following problem for all students to see:

$\frac{3}{4}$ of a brown rod $- \frac{1}{4}$ of a brown rod =
_____ brown rod

4. Students should have no trouble stating that the answer is $\frac{2}{4}$ (or $\frac{1}{2}$) of a brown rod. Acknowledge this is correct, but then ask how they could use the rods to prove to someone else that both answers—$\frac{2}{4}$ of a brown rod and $\frac{1}{2}$ of a brown rod—are correct and are, in fact, the same thing.

5. Encourage students to use what they know about fractional relationships to find three of the rods that are $\frac{1}{4}$ as long as the brown rod, lay them end to end, and show them if they remove or cover up one of the $\frac{1}{4}$, they have $\frac{2}{4}$ (or $\frac{1}{2}$) left.

This illustrates Strategy #10 of the ten essential strategies for supporting fraction sense: *Provide opportunities for students to build on their reasoning and sense-making skills about fractions by working with a variety of manipulatives and tools, such as Cuisenaire rods, Pattern Blocks, Fraction Kits, and ordinary items from their lives.* To learn more about this strategy, see Chapter 1 of *Beyond Pizzas & Pies: 10 Essential Strategies for Supporting Fraction Sense, Grades 3–5, Second Edition* (McNamara and Shaughnessy 2015).

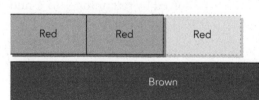

6. After students come to a consensus that the rods prove that $\frac{3}{4}$ of a brown rod minus $\frac{1}{4}$ of a brown rod does, indeed, equal $\frac{2}{4}$ (or $\frac{1}{2}$) of a brown rod, display the following problem for all students to see:

$$1\frac{3}{8}\ \text{brown rod} - \frac{1}{8}\ \text{brown rod} =$$
_____ brown rod(s)

This illustrates Strategy #3 of the ten essential strategies for supporting fraction sense: *Provide opportunities for students to recognize equivalent fractions as different ways to name the same quantity.* To learn more about this strategy, see Chapter 1 of *Beyond Pizzas & Pies: 10 Essential Strategies for Supporting Fraction Sense, Grades 3–5, Second Edition* (McNamara and Shaughnessy 2015).

7. Students are again likely to answer that $1\frac{3}{8}$ of a brown rod minus $\frac{1}{8}$ of a brown rod equals $1\frac{2}{8}$ (or $1\frac{1}{4}$) of a brown rod. Again, ask how they could use the rods to prove that both answers are correct. Students may be content to answer that two of the white rods are the same length as the red rod, which they already know is $\frac{1}{4}$ of the brown rod. Press them to explain again how they know the red rod is $\frac{1}{4}$ the length of the brown rod.

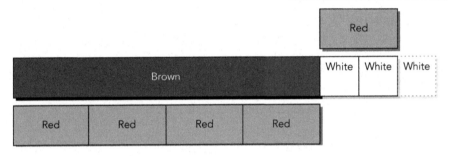

8. Next display the following problem for all students to see:

$$\frac{7}{8}\ \text{brown rod} - \frac{1}{4}\ \text{brown rod} = \underline{\hspace{3cm}}\ \text{brown rod(s)}$$

9. Some students may subtract across numerators and denominators and suggest that the answer is $\frac{6}{4}$; others may not know how to proceed at all. If no one suggests it, ask if there is a way they could use equivalent fractions to determine how to subtract $\frac{1}{4}$ from $\frac{7}{8}$. Ask if either fraction could be renamed so the two fractions have the same denominator.

> ### Teaching Tip
> It may be tempting to create a chart that identifies the fractional relationships among the rods before beginning this activity. It is more beneficial for students, however, to use the definition of a fraction to determine these relationships in the context of solving problems such as the ones included here.

10. Guide students to see that the red rod is also the same length as two white rods, and because one white rod is $\frac{1}{8}$ of the brown rod, the problem could be solved by renaming $\frac{1}{4}$ to $\frac{2}{8}$ and subtracting $\frac{2}{8}$ from $\frac{7}{8}$, equaling $\frac{5}{8}$.

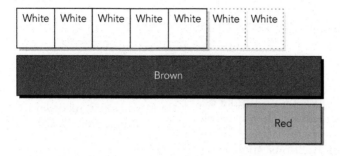

11. Next, display the following problem for all students to see:

$1\frac{1}{2}$ brown rod – $\frac{3}{4}$ brown rod = _____ brown rod(s)

12. Students will likely realize that the difference is less than one brown rod, but may not know how to complete the subtraction. Ask if either fraction could be renamed to make the subtraction possible. Students may first rename $1\frac{1}{2}$ as $\frac{3}{2}$. If so, ask again if $\frac{3}{2}$ could be renamed to make it possible to subtract $\frac{3}{4}$.

13. Encourage students to use the rods to see that $1\frac{1}{2}$ (or $\frac{3}{2}$) can be renamed as $\frac{6}{4}$ to subtract $\frac{3}{4}$.

14. In addition, some students may use the "Get to the Whole" strategy from Chapter 3 to subtract $\frac{2}{4}$ from $1\frac{1}{2}$, to arrive at 1, and then take one more $\frac{1}{4}$ from 1 to get the answer $\frac{3}{4}$. If so, make sure to encourage them to describe the renaming they use to arrive at their answer. For example, they were able to subtract $\frac{2}{4}$ from $1\frac{1}{2}$ because they know that $\frac{2}{4}$ is equivalent to $\frac{1}{2}$, and then they were able to take $\frac{1}{4}$ from 1 because they know that 1 is equivalent to $\frac{4}{4}$.

15. Pass out the *Subtraction with Cuisenaire Rods*, Version 1, recording sheet and have students work in pairs or independently to solve the problems. (See Figure 4–1; also available as Reproducible 4a.) Monitor as students complete the problems and take note of which problems are especially challenging. When students have completed the sheet, have a few students share their strategies for solving the problems that seemed to engender the most discussion and problem solving.

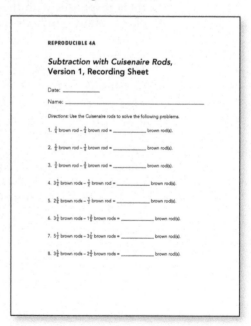

Figure 4–1. *Subtraction with Cuisenaire Rods*, Version 1, recording sheet

4.2 Subtraction with Cuisenaire Rods, Version 2

Overview

As in Version 1, students use Cuisenaire rods to subtract fractions with unlike denominators. Unlike Version 1, the whole changes in each problem, thus helping students learn that fractions such as $\frac{1}{2}$ and $\frac{4}{5}$ are not names for specific rods, but rather descriptions of relationships between the rod designated as the part and the rod length designated as the whole.

<table>
<tr><td>Materials</td></tr>
<tr><td>Subtraction with Cuisenaire Rods, Version 2, recording sheet (Reproducible 4b), 1 per student

Cuisenaire rods, 1 set per pair of students</td></tr>
</table>

1. If students have completed *Subtraction with Cuisenaire Rods*, Version 1, tell them that *Subtraction with Cuisenaire Rods*, Version 2, involves similar problems, but instead of always using the brown rod as the whole, each problem uses a different rod. Depending on your students, you may want to have them work independently or with a partner to solve the first problem, and then process their responses with the whole class. Many students may be hesitant to use the red rod to represent $\frac{1}{5}$ of the orange rod because it was used as $\frac{1}{4}$ of the brown rod in Version 1. This is a perfect time to revisit and reinforce what it means for something to be $\frac{1}{5}$ (or $\frac{1}{2}$ or $\frac{1}{8}$ or $\frac{1}{n}$) of something else. Pass out the *Subtraction with Cuisenaire Rods*, Version 2, recording sheet so students can record their solutions. (See Figure 4–2; also available as Reproducible 4b.)

This illustrates Strategy #4 of the ten essential strategies for supporting fraction sense: *Provide opportunities for students to work with changing units.* To learn more about this strategy, see Chapter 1 of *Beyond Pizzas & Pies: 10 Essential Strategies for Supporting Fraction Sense, Grades 3–5, Second Edition* (McNamara and Shaughnessy 2015).

REPRODUCIBLE 4B

Subtraction with Cuisenaire Rods, Version 2, Recording Sheet

Date: _____

Name: _____

Directions: Use the Cuisenaire rods to solve the following problems.

1. $\frac{4}{5}$ orange rod – $\frac{2}{5}$ orange rod = _____ orange rod(s).

2. $\frac{3}{4}$ purple rod – $\frac{1}{2}$ purple rod = _____ purple rod(s).

3. $1\frac{2}{3}$ dark green rods – $\frac{5}{6}$ dark green rod = _____ dark green rod(s).

4. 5 red rods – $1\frac{1}{2}$ red rods = _____ red rod(s).

5. $4\frac{1}{2}$ orange rods – $2\frac{4}{5}$ orange rods = _____ orange rod(s).

6. $2\frac{1}{2}$ dark green rods – $1\frac{1}{3}$ dark green rods = _____ dark green rod(s).

7. $2\frac{1}{2}$ orange rods – $1\frac{4}{5}$ orange rods = _____ orange rod(s).

8. $5\frac{1}{3}$ dark green rods – $3\frac{1}{2}$ dark green rods = _____ dark green rod(s).

Figure 4–2. *Subtraction with Cuisenaire Rods*, Version 2, recording sheet

4.3 *What's the Difference?*

Materials
What's the Difference?, recording sheet (**Reproducible 4c**), 1 per student

Overview

In this activity, students use number lines to solve *Compare* problems by finding the difference between two values.

1. Display the following problem for all students to see:

> *On Monday night Wendy spent $\frac{1}{2}$ an hour on her math homework. On Tuesday night she spent $\frac{3}{4}$ of an hour on her math homework. How much longer did Wendy spend on her homework on Tuesday night than on Monday night?*

2. Allow time for students to read the problem and discuss what the problem is about. After students understand the context and the question, ask, "How might we use a number line to represent the two quantities and answer the question?"[1]

3. Display a number line like the one shown here. Make the unit interval (1 hour) explicit. On top of the number line, draw a line to represent the time Wendy spent on math homework on Monday night. Below the line, draw a line to represent the time Wendy spent on math homework on Tuesday night.

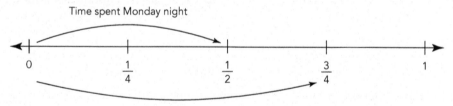

Time spent Monday night

Time spent Tuesday night

---

[1] Different students are likely to use the number line for different purposes. For students who aren't able to determine the difference readily between $\frac{1}{2}$ and $\frac{3}{4}$, the number line can serve as a tool to help them find the answer. Van Den Heuvel-Panhuizen (2003) refers to this as using the number line as a "representation" for thinking. Other students who are able to determine the difference between $\frac{1}{2}$ and $\frac{3}{4}$ mentally should be encouraged to use the number line to show the mathematics behind their answer.

4. Indicate the difference between the times Wendy spent on math home-work on the two nights by using an arrow or highlighter.

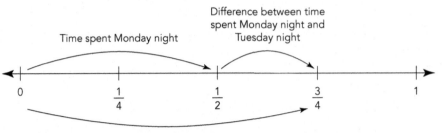

5. If no one suggests it during the discussion, make sure students realize the difference can be found by adding up from $\frac{1}{2}$ or by subtracting back from $\frac{3}{4}$. Both strategies work; the decision of which one to use is often dependent on the numbers involved.

6. Present the next problem and provide time for students to discuss the context and the question:

Kira's favorite cookie recipe needs $1\frac{1}{3}$ cups of sugar. Jeremy's favorite cookie recipe needs $\frac{2}{3}$ of a cup of sugar. How much more sugar does Kira's recipe need than Jeremy's?

7. After it is clear that everyone understands the problem, again ask, "How might we use a number line to represent the two quantities and answer the question?"

8. Allow students time to solve the problem. If they are able to solve the problem independently or with a partner, allow volunteers to show how they used a number line to represent and solve the problem.

9. If students are not yet independent, repeat the process described earlier, using a number line to show the amount of sugar Kira's recipe needs and the amount of sugar Jeremy's recipe needs.

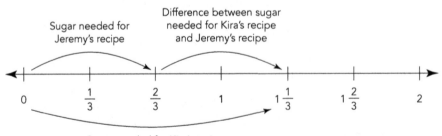

10. As students work on additional problems, it may not be necessary for them to draw lines showing the two values being compared. In this case, allow students to indicate the values by showing them on the number line as shown here.

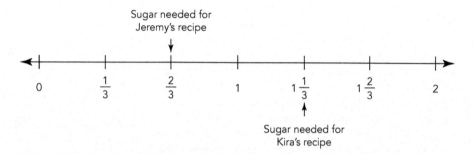

11. For additional practice with *Compare* problems, have students complete *What's the Difference?* (See Figure 4–3; also available as Reproducible 4c.)

REPRODUCIBLE 4C

What's the Difference?, Recording Sheet

Date: _____

Name: _____

Directions: Use the number line to solve each problem.

1. Kira's favorite cookie recipe needs 1⅓ cups of sugar. Jeremy's favorite cookie recipe needs ⅔ of a cup of sugar. How much more sugar does Kira's recipe need than Jeremy's?

2. Mariah and Grace are comparing how much they ran over the weekend to get in shape for soccer season. Mariah ran 4⅚ of a mile. Grace ran 3¼ of a mile. How much farther did Mariah run than Grace?

3. Frankie walks ⅞ of a mile to school. Albert walks ⅔ of a mile to school. How much farther does Albert walk than Frankie?

4. Mr. Gregory is making his costume for the class play. The jacket needs 2⅓ yards of fabric and the pants need 1⅔ yards of fabric. How much more fabric does the jacket need than the pants?

5. Erik is working on his long jump. The school record is 10½ feet. Erik can jump 8¼ feet. How many feet is Erik from matching the record?

Figure 4–3. *What's the Difference?,* recording sheet

4.4

Tell Me All You Can, Subtraction

Materials
none

Overview

The activity *Tell Me All You Can* (adapted from Bresser and Holzman [2006]) can be used in any content area and is especially helpful when addressing content or concepts that may look somewhat new to students. Students are shown a problem such as $5\frac{1}{6} - 1\frac{3}{8}$ and are told to look closely at the numbers and operations involved. Before coming up with an exact answer, students are to consider and discuss everything they know about the problem as a means of getting a sense of the "neighborhood" of the answer. Problems can be chosen to highlight specific strategies, such as estimation and the use of benchmarks, as well as to bring to light common challenges and misconceptions students often have.

> This illustrates Strategy #9 of the ten essential strategies for supporting fraction sense: *Provide opportunities for students to engage in mathematical discourse and share and discuss their mathematical ideas, even those that may not be fully formed or completely accurate.* To learn more about this strategy, see Chapter 1 of *Beyond Pizzas & Pies: 10 Essential Strategies for Supporting Fraction Sense, Grades 3–5*, Second Edition (McNamara and Shaughnessy 2015).

1. Begin by displaying the problem $\frac{3}{4} - \frac{1}{2}$ and tell students you don't want them to give you an exact answer. Instead, you want them to "tell you all they can" about the answer. If students have trouble coming up with ideas, the following sentence frames may help them get started:

- The answer will be more than _____ because _____.
  (*The answer will be more than 0 because $\frac{3}{4} - \frac{3}{4} = 0$, and $\frac{1}{2}$ is less than $\frac{3}{4}$.*)

- The answer will be less than _____ because _____.
  (*The answer will be less than $\frac{1}{2}$ because $\frac{3}{4}$ is less than 1, and $1 - \frac{1}{2} = \frac{1}{2}$.*)

- The answer will be between _____ and _____ because _____.
  (*The answer will be between 0 and $\frac{1}{2}$, because we're subtracting more than $\frac{1}{4}$ [which would get us to $\frac{1}{2}$], but less than $\frac{3}{4}$ [which would get us to 0].*)

2. You may also ask students questions such as, "Will the answer be more or less than $\frac{1}{2}$? How do you know?" and "Will the answer be more or less than 0? How do you know?"

3. Tell students to turn and talk to their neighbor or elbow partner and share their ideas about the answer.

4. When students have had adequate time to discuss the problem with their partner, ask for volunteers to share an idea (either one they thought of or one they heard from their partner) with the whole class.

5. Chart students' contributions, and be sure to ask students for their rationale if they do not provide it without prompting.

6. Display another problem and repeat the process.

7. Suggestions for addressing different problem types are as follows:

Subtracting fractions with like denominators:

$1\frac{1}{3} - \frac{2}{3}$: The answer will be less than 1 because $1\frac{1}{3} - \frac{1}{3} = 1$, and we're subtracting another $\frac{1}{3}$. The answer will be more than $\frac{1}{2}$ because we are subtracting $\frac{1}{3}$ from 1 (after subtracting the first $\frac{1}{3}$), and $\frac{1}{3}$ is less than $\frac{1}{2}$.

Subtracting fractions with unlike denominators:

$\frac{7}{8} - \frac{2}{3}$: The answer will be less than $\frac{1}{2}$ because $\frac{7}{8} - \frac{3}{8} = \frac{4}{8}$ (or $\frac{1}{2}$), and $\frac{2}{3}$ is more than $\frac{3}{8}$.

$\frac{3}{4} - \frac{1}{6}$: The answer will be more than $\frac{1}{2}$ because $\frac{3}{4} - \frac{1}{4} = \frac{1}{2}$, and $\frac{1}{6}$ is less than $\frac{1}{4}$.

Subtracting mixed numbers:

$4\frac{1}{6} - 1\frac{5}{12}$: The answer will be more than $2\frac{1}{6}$ because $4\frac{1}{6} - 2$ equals $2\frac{1}{6}$, and $1\frac{5}{12}$ is less than 2. The answer will be less than 3 because we're taking away more than $1\frac{1}{6}$.

The understanding that subtraction problems with fractions can be solved by using a *Separate* (or take-away) strategy, a counting up strategy, or by comparing both values is an essential aspect of understanding operations with fractions. As students use this knowledge to solve fraction subtraction problems they are deepening their conceptual understanding and developing strategies for fraction subtraction that are flexible and responsive to the numbers and contexts involved. In addition, by using their knowledge of equivalent fractions to subtract fractions with unlike denominators, students strengthen and use their understanding that equivalent fractions are different ways of naming the same number. In this way, students' strategies for fraction subtraction "build on previous understandings" as called for in the Common Core State Standards for Mathematics.

Study Questions

After Reading Chapter 4

1. What information presented in the "Classroom Scenario," "What's the Math?," and "What's the Research?" sections was familiar to you or similar to your experience with students?

2. Using one's knowledge of equivalent fractions to subtract fractions with unlike denominators is a somewhat different approach to subtracting fractions than we have seen in the past (finding common denominators). How will this change influence how you approach subtracting fractions with your students?

3. Which of the Classroom Activities (Activity 4.1, *Subtraction with Cuisenaire Rods*, Version 1; Activity 4.2, *Subtraction with Cuisenaire Rods*, Version 2; Activity 4.3, *What's the Difference?*; Activity 4.4, *Tell Me All You Can*) do you plan to implement with your students?

After Trying One or More of the Activities

1. Describe the activity and any modifications you made to meet your students' needs or to align with your curriculum.

2. How did this activity add to your knowledge of what your students do and do not understand about subtracting fractions?

3. What are your next steps for supporting your students' learning about subtracting fractions?

Connections with *Beyond Pizzas & Pies, Second Edition*

Beyond Invert & Multiply builds on the foundational understandings introduced in its companion resource, *Beyond Pizzas & Pies, Second Edition*. I recommend pairing this chapter with Chapters 3 and 4 in *Beyond Pizzas & Pies* to continue your learning.

Multiplication and Division with Fractions

Developing Awareness

Multiplication and Division Problem Types

OUTLINE

To understand the complexity of multiplication and division of fractions, it is essential that students understand these operations with whole numbers. Much like addition and subtraction (discussed in Chapter 2), understanding multiplication and division involves far more than just the ability to perform calculations accurately. Students need to be able to make sense of mathematical situations to determine which operation is called for, and then know what the resulting answers represent. In addition, understanding the relationship between multiplication and division is essential, particularly as students use a standard algorithm for dividing fractions, such as "invert and multiply" (discussed in detail in Chapter 7).

Contexts and representations can support students' understanding of the meaning of multiplication and division of fractions, and can help them extend their thinking beyond the specific context being used to a more generalized understanding that focuses on mathematical relationships (Fosnot and Dolk 2002). It is essential, however, that the representations used match the context of a given situation. For example, to support students' understanding of fractions as numbers on the number line, contexts that involve time and distance can be represented with linear models such as Cuisenaire rods and number lines. Area models can also be used to represent fraction multiplication and division, but should be used in situations that address area or arrays specifically, such as the cupcake problem presented later. Wyberg et al. (2012) found that folding waxed hamburger patty papers provided a strong visual model for helping students understand multiplying fractions.

When presenting students with contextualized fraction multiplication and division problems (or word problems), it is just as important to consider the problem situations to which students are exposed, as it is when students are working with whole numbers. Students need opportunities to grapple with and make sense of various problem types and to interpret the results of their calculations.

> " When presenting students with contextualized fraction multiplication and division problems (or word problems), it is just as important to consider the problem situations to which students are exposed.

A great deal of research has gone into identifying types of multiplication and division situations, as well as understanding how students approach different problem types (Carpenter et al. 1999). When students first encounter multiplication and division situations, the situations are of the grouping and partitioning type. An example is shown here:

Ms. Jones has 3 prep periods per week. Each prep period is 45 minutes long. Ms. Jones has 135 minutes of prep time per week.

Problems can be written so that any one of the quantities is the unknown. For example, if the total number of minutes (135) is the unknown, it is a multiplication problem. If the length of each prep period (45 minutes) is the unknown, it is a partitive division problem. If the number of prep periods per week (3) is the unknown, it is a quotative (also called *measurement*) division problem.

The Common Core State Standards for Mathematics (CCSSM) identifies three distinct problem situations—*Equal Groups*, *Arrays/Area*, and *Compare*—within the three problem types (multiplication, partitive division, and quotative division) just mentioned. (See Table 5–1 for a summary of the different problem situations.)

Like addition and subtraction problems, the same equation can be used to find an answer to different problem types, but students may find the different

Table 5–1. Multiplication and Division Problem Situations

	Multiplication (product unknown)	Quotative Division (number of groups unknown)	Partitive Division (group size unknown)
Equal Groups	Mr. Vargas has 6 days to complete his conferences. *If he does 8 conferences each day, how many conferences will Mr. Vargas complete in total?*	Mr. Vargas is able to complete 8 conferences each day. *If he does 48 conferences in all, how many days will he need to complete his conferences?*	Mr. Vargas has 6 days to complete his conferences. *If he does 48 conferences in all, how many conferences will he complete each day?*
Arrays/ Area	Mr. Vargas made cupcakes for his class. He arranged them in 6 rows with 8 cupcakes per row. *How many cupcakes did Mr. Vargas make?*	Mr. Vargas made 48 cupcakes for his class. He arranged them in rows of 8. *How many rows of cupcakes did Mr. Vargas make?*	Mr. Vargas made 48 cupcakes for his class. He arranged them in 6 rows. *How many cupcakes did Mr. Vargas put in each row?*

(continued)

Table 5–1. *Continued.*

	Multiplication (product unknown)	Quotative Division (number of groups unknown)	Partitive Division (group size unknown)
Compare	Last year, Mr. Vargas's students were able to collect 8 bags of books for the book drive. This year's students collected 6 times as many bags. *How many bags of books did this year's students collect?*	This year, Mr. Vargas's students were able to collect 48 bags of books for the book drive. Last year's students were only able to collect 8 bags of books. *How many times more bags of books did this year's students collect than last year's?*	This year, Mr. Vargas's students were able to collect 48 bags of books for the book drive. This is 6 times as many bags as last year's students. *How many bags of books did last year's students collect?*

Source: Adapted from NGA Center and the CCSSO (2010).

problem types more or less difficult to solve depending on the context involved. Here are three problems that can all be solved by the equation $6 \times 8 = 48$:

- *Equal Groups:* Mr. Vargas has 6 days to complete his conferences. If he does 8 conferences each day, how many conferences will Mr. Vargas complete in total?
- *Arrays/Area:* Mr. Vargas made cupcakes for his class. He arranged them in 6 rows with 8 cupcakes per row. How many cupcakes did Mr. Vargas make?
- *Compare:* Last year, Mr. Vargas's students were able to collect 8 bags of books for the book drive. This year's students collected 6 times as many bags. How many bags of books did this year's students collect?

By rewriting each problem so that either of the other values are the unknown, the problems become division situations. Partitive division refers to problems in which the group size is unknown; quotative division refers to problems in which the number of groups is unknown. Examples of each type follow.

PARTITIVE DIVISION

- *Equal Groups:* Mr. Vargas has 6 days to complete his conferences. If he does 48 conferences in all, how many conferences will he complete each day?
- *Arrays/Area:* Mr. Vargas made 48 cupcakes for his class. He arranged them in 6 rows. How many cupcakes did Mr. Vargas put in each row?
- *Compare:* This year, Mr. Vargas's students were able to collect 48 bags of books for the book drive. This is 6 times as many bags as last year's students. How many bags of books did last year's students collect?

QUOTATIVE DIVISION

- *Equal Groups:* Mr. Vargas is able to complete 8 conferences each day. If he does 48 conferences in all, how many days will he need to complete his conferences?
- *Arrays/Area:* Mr. Vargas made 48 cupcakes for his class. He arranged them in rows of 8. How many rows of cupcakes did Mr. Vargas make?
- *Compare:* This year, Mr. Vargas's students were able to collect 48 bags of books for the book drive. Last year's students were only able to collect 8 bags of books. How many times more bags of books did this year's students collect than last year's?

Students often have an easier time solving quotative division problems than partitive division problems because they can use repeated subtraction to find the quotient. Although repeated subtraction can be used to solve partitive division problems and arrive at a correct answer, the resulting groupings do not accurately represent the problem as presented. The following is an example which uses the conference problem to illustrate the situation.

Quotative Division: Mr. Vargas is able to complete 8 conferences each day. If he does 48 conferences in all, how many days will he need to complete his conferences?

Total number of conferences	48	40	32	24	16	8
Conferences each day	8	8	8	8	8	8
	Day 1	Day 2	Day 3	Day 4	Day 5	Day 6

When presenting the same context as a partitive division problem, the use of repeated subtraction does not match the context. Although one can subtract 6 from 48 repeatedly and arrive at 8, this particular problem entails subtracting days from conferences, which doesn't make sense. Because the number of groups (or the number of days for completing his conferences) is known, and the number in each group (or the number of conferences completed each day) is the unknown, students often solve partitive division problems by using a dealing-out strategy. Given the conference problem, students might start by identifying the 6 days and then dealing out the conferences one at a time until all 48 are distributed evenly. Only after this task is complete is it possible for students to find there are 8 conferences completed each day.

In Summary

Although the research on multiplication and division problem types, and students' approaches to solving them, is based on work with whole numbers, the same ideas apply when students transition to computations with fractions. To support students to be successful with multiplication and division of fractions, it is important to keep in mind (1) there are many different types of problem situations, (2) students find different types of problem situations more or less difficult to solve, and (3) problems that can be solved with the same equation may look very different to students.

> **It is important to keep in mind (1) there are many different types of problem situations, (2) students find different types of problem situations more or less difficult to solve, and (3) problems that can be solved with the same equation may look very different to students.**

As with whole number computation, students need multiple opportunities to consider computation with fractions through solving a variety of problem types. Such opportunities enable students to approach fraction multiplication and division from a sense-making point of view, instead of simply trying to computer without considering what the numbers in the problems mean. It is important to note that many of the problems in the following chapters are presented without contexts. This is not an oversight, but rather an intentional decision to provide opportunities for students to reason about fractions as numbers outside of a specific context. Although contexts can, and should, be used to help students to make sense of operations and to check their results for reasonableness, students need to be able to manipulate fractions and perform calculations context free. As stated in the Common Core State Standards for Mathematics:

> Mathematically proficient students have . . . the ability to decontextualize—to abstract a given situation and represent it symbolically and manipulate the representing symbols as if they have a life of their own, without necessarily attending to their referents—and the ability to contextualize, to pause as needed during the manipulation process in order to probe into the referents for the symbols involved. (NGA Center/CCSSO 2010, 6)

Study Questions

After Reading Chapter 5

1. What information presented in the "What's the Context?" and "What's the Research?" sections was familiar to you or similar to your experience with students?

2. How might you use knowledge of different multiplication and division problem types to support your students' understanding of multiplication and division with fractions?

Making Sense
Multiplication with Fractions

OUTLINE

CCSS Connections

Prerequisite Standards

3.NF.A.1: Understand a fraction 1/b as the quantity formed by 1 part when a whole is partitioned into b equal parts; understand a fraction a/b as the quantity formed by a parts of size 1/b.

Standards Addressed

4.NF.B.3: Understand a fraction a/b with a > 1 as a sum of fractions 1/b.

4.NF.B.4: Apply and extend previous understandings of multiplication to multiply a fraction by a whole number.

5.NF.B.4: Apply and extend previous understandings of multiplication to multiply a fraction or whole number by a fraction.

5.NF.B.6: Solve real-world problems involving multiplication of fractions and mixed numbers.

Ms. Chu's fifth graders were creating an All School Sports Day to celebrate their completion of elementary school, and were applying their learning to contexts outside of the classroom. One of the events was a mile run, which they mapped out around the school's neighborhood. A few students were worried that the younger kids would need encouragement to keep going for the full mile, so they spent some time discussing how to keep them motivated after their first burst of energy wore off. Willie told his classmates that when he and his mom ran the Bay to Breakers race in San Francisco, the mile marker signs really helped to keep him motivated. After a brief discussion, the students decided they would make signs to mark each quarter mile, then post themselves at intervals that were one-fourth the distance of each quarter mile to give high fives and cheers as the younger students passed.

While the students were working in groups on the signs for the quarter mile markers, Ms. Chu came across a group that had decided to make smaller signs to mark the ends of each of the smaller intervals as well. As she approached the table, she overheard Zoe suggesting that they put the distance traveled on each of the signs—just like the mile markers in the Bay to Breakers.

"How do we figure out what to put on each sign?" Mai asked. "I mean, we can't write '*Woohoo! One mile completed*' until they get all the way to the end of the run."

"We have to figure out what fraction of the mile they will have traveled at each marker and put that on the sign," explained Willie patiently.

"We know that the signs at the quarter-mile marks will say '*One-fourth of a mile completed*,' '*Two-fourths of a mile completed*,' and '*Three-fourths of a mile completed*,'" Ari continued.

"I think we have to figure out what's one-fourth of one-fourth, but I'm really not sure how we do that," Willie said, looking to Zoe. "What do you think? It sounds like we need to divide one-fourth by one-fourth because we're dividing up the quarter-mile sections into smaller sections."

"I was thinking that too," Zoe began, "but now I'm not so sure."

"Me too. For some reason I'm thinking that *of*, as in one-fourth *of* one-fourth means multiply but that doesn't seem to make much sense," Ari responded.

"Oh! On the 'Two-fourths of a mile' sign we should also write '*One-half of a mile completed*' to include equivalent fractions! Ms. Chu will like that," Mai, who often contributed very astute comments a few beats behind her more verbal classmates, interrupted with a grin.

"That's a great idea Mai, and we all know Ms. Chu will like that," Willie said while Ari and Zoe nodded in agreement. "But we still don't know what goes on the other signs."

Ms. Chu smiled to herself as the students continued their conversation and considered whether she should interject or let them continue without her input. She knew the students were somewhat stumped, but she also knew that by inserting herself into the conversation too soon she ran the risk of preventing her students from achieving the deep understanding that often resulted from this kind of "constructive struggling."[1] She also noticed that Zoe had taken out a sheet of scratch paper on which she had drawn out the track and written $\frac{1}{4} \times \frac{1}{4} = \frac{1}{16}$. Ms. Chu decided to listen a bit longer and see how the conversation unfolded.

"The smaller signs will be one-fourth of the way to the quarter-mile markers, so each small sign will be at the end of one-sixteenth of a mile," Zoe began. "I drew it out and I also multiplied one-fourth by one-fourth and got one-sixteenth."

The rest of the students looked at Zoe's picture and indicated agreement with her placement of the signs.

"OK, I get why you show that there will be sixteen signs if we include the ones at the quarter-mile marks and the final one at the end," Willie began, in his frequent role as spokesman for the group. "But what I don't get is how you got one-sixteenth when you multiplied one-fourth times one-fourth."

"Yeah, me too," Ari and Mai said at the same time.

"One-sixteenth is way smaller than one-fourth, right?" Willie continued. As the other students nodded agreement, Ms. Chu thought she knew exactly where Willie was headed. "So it just doesn't make sense. I mean, multiplication always make things bigger. Doesn't it?"

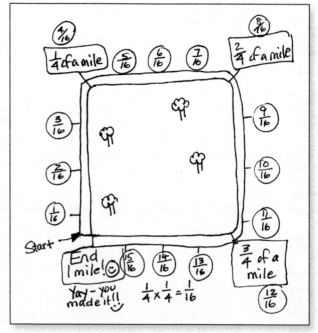

Zoe's illustration of the track.

> So it just doesn't make sense. I mean, multiplication always make things bigger. Doesn't it?

---

[1] *Constructive struggling* is a term used by Cathy Seeley in her book *Faster Isn't Smarter* (2009) to describe the kind of struggle that is at the right level of challenge so it is both "constructive and instructive."

When students first encounter multiplication, they are often taught that multiplication is the same as repeated addition and that, when given two factors and a product in the form of a "fact family," the product is always the largest of the three numbers. Although these approaches can be helpful for students when working with whole numbers, they can lead students to incorrect generalizations such as the one expressed by Willie in the classroom scenario on the previous page. In addition, to help students compute with efficiency, they are often encouraged to make generalizations without sufficient qualifiers, such as, "The answer to a multiplication problem is larger than either factor *when both factors are greater than one.*"

An Alternative to Repeated Addition

Approaching fractions from a measurement approach can also be useful when addressing fraction multiplication. An example using whole numbers can help to illustrate. Given the problem *4 × 3*, if one considers a multiunit length of 4, iterated three times, or (using the commutative property) a multiunit length of 3 iterated four times, one arrives at 12. This could be thought of as "four iterations of length 3" or "three iterations of length 4" or the shorter "four *of* 3" or "three *of* 4." (See Figures 6–1 and 6–2.)

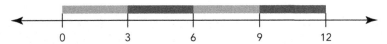

Figure 6–1. 4 × 3, or four of 3.

Figure 6–2. 3 × 4, or three of 4.

This same strategy can be used with the problem $4 \times \frac{1}{3}$, which could be considered as four iterations of the subunit length $\frac{1}{3}$ or one-third of an iteration of the multiunit length of 4. Four iterations of $\frac{1}{3}$ is generally quite simple to illustrate (See Figure 6–3.)

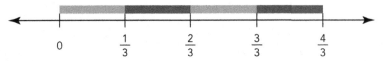

Figure 6–3. $4 \times \frac{1}{3}$, or four of $\frac{1}{3}$.

To illustrate $\frac{1}{3}$ of length 4 ($\frac{1}{3} \times 4$), however, we need to return to the meaning of $\frac{1}{3}$. Recall that, according to the measurement model, a length, distance, quantity, or area is $\frac{1}{3}$ of a referent if three exact copies or iterations of said model, length, distance, quantity, or area equal the referent. For example, 5 is $\frac{1}{3}$ of 15 because three 5s equal 15. By the same token, twenty minutes is $\frac{1}{3}$ of an hour because three periods of time each equaling twenty minutes is equivalent to one hour.

To find $\frac{1}{3}$ of length 4, we need to determine the length that, when iterated three times, equals 4. We can do this by partitioning length 4 into three equal subsections, each of which is $\frac{1}{3}$ of length 4. We now need to determine the value of the subsections, which we know is somewhere between 1 and 2. Using the measurement approach, and what we know about number lines, we determine that the fractional part of the subsection is equal to $\frac{1}{3}$ of the unit interval, because its length, when iterated three times, is the same as the unit interval. We can now determine that the length that is $\frac{1}{3}$ of length 4 is, in fact, $1\frac{1}{3}$, the same length we found when we iterated $\frac{1}{3}$ four times. (See Figure 6–4.)

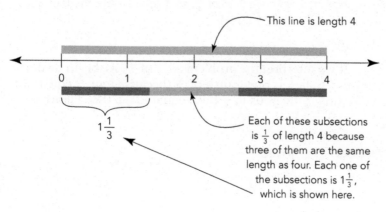

Figure 6–4. $\frac{1}{3} \times 4$, or $\frac{1}{3}$ of 4

The measurement approach can also be used when multiplying a fraction by a fraction, such as $\frac{2}{3} \times \frac{3}{4}$ or $\frac{3}{4} \times \frac{2}{3}$. As discussed in Chapter 3, Making Sense: Addition with Fractions, understanding that $\frac{2}{3}$ is made up of two parts of $\frac{1}{3}$, and $\frac{3}{4}$ is made up of three parts of $\frac{1}{4}$, is an essential aspect of understanding fractions as numbers (CCSS 3.NF.A.1). To determine the value of $\frac{2}{3} \times \frac{3}{4}$, we first need to determine the value of $\frac{1}{3}$ of $\frac{3}{4}$. Again, a number line is a useful tool for doing so. (See Figure 6–5.)

See also Chapter 3, Making Sense: Addition with Fractions.

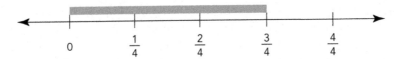

Figure 6–5. $\frac{3}{4}$ on the number line

Using the definition of $\frac{1}{3}$ discussed here and in Chapter 1, *Making Sense: Fractions as Numbers,* we can see that $\frac{1}{4}$ is one-third of $\frac{3}{4}$, because three $\frac{1}{4}$s is equal to $\frac{3}{4}$. (See Figure 6–6.)

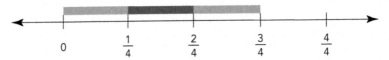

Figure 6–6. This figure shows that $\frac{1}{4}$ is one-third of $\frac{3}{4}$, so $\frac{2}{4}$ (or $\frac{1}{2}$) is two-thirds of $\frac{3}{4}$. It also shows that two-thirds of $\frac{3}{4}$ is then $\frac{2}{4}$ (or $\frac{1}{2}$).

See also Chapter 1, **Making Sense: Fractions as Numbers.**

If we interpret the problem as $\frac{3}{4}$ of $\frac{2}{3}$, we begin by determining that $\frac{1}{6}$ is one-fourth of $\frac{2}{3}$ (because four $\frac{1}{6}$ equals $\frac{2}{3}$), and three $\frac{1}{6}$ takes us to $\frac{3}{6}$ (also equal to $\frac{1}{2}$). (See Figure 6–7.)

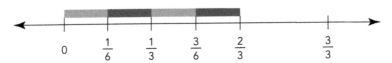

Figure 6–7. The number line shows that $\frac{1}{6}$ is one-fourth of $\frac{2}{3}$, so $\frac{3}{6}$ (or $\frac{1}{2}$) is three-fourths of $\frac{2}{3}$.

An area model can also be used to represent fraction multiplication. To show the product of $\frac{2}{3} \times \frac{3}{4}$ using an area model, we begin with a square with side lengths of one partitioned horizontally into thirds, then shade two of the thirds. (See Figure 6–8.)

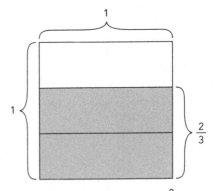

Figure 6–8. Area model with $\frac{2}{3}$ shaded.

We then partition the shaded $\frac{2}{3}$ of the square into fourths, and doubly-shade three of the fourths. (See Figure 6–9.)

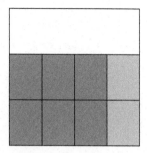

Figure 6–9. Area model showing $\frac{3}{4} \times \frac{2}{3}$.

To determine what part of the total square is now shaded, we can partition the square further to make all the sections of equal size. By doing so, we see the square is partitioned into twelfths and six of the twelfths are doubly-shaded. Based on our understanding of equivalent fractions, we determine that $\frac{6}{12}$ is equivalent to $\frac{1}{2}$. (See Figure 6–10.)

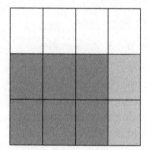

Figure 6–10. Area model showing that $\frac{3}{4} \times \frac{2}{3} = \frac{6}{12} = \frac{1}{2}$.

We can repeat the entire process previously discussed by starting with the original square partitioned and shaded to show $\frac{3}{4}$. (See Figure 6–11.)

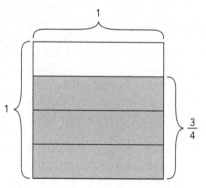

Figure 6–11. Area model with $\frac{3}{4}$ shaded.

We then partition the shaded $\frac{3}{4}$ of the square into thirds, and doubly-shaded two of the thirds. (See Figure 6–12.)

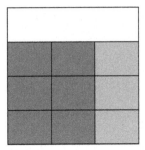

Figure 6–12. Area model showing $\frac{2}{3} \times \frac{3}{4}$.

To determine what part of the total square is now shaded, we can partition the square further to make all of the sections of equal size. By doing so, we see that the square is partitioned into twelfths and six of the twelfths are doubly-shaded. Based on our understanding of equivalent fractions, we determine that $\frac{6}{12}$ is equivalent to $\frac{1}{2}$. (See Figure 6–13.)

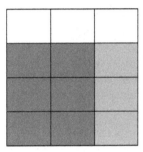

Figure 6–13. Area model showing that $\frac{2}{3} \times \frac{3}{4} = \frac{6}{12} = \frac{1}{2}$.

Multiplication as Scaling

In addition to thinking of multiplication as repeated addition (which has limitations) and measurement (which can be difficult to consider, depending on the numbers involved), multiplication can also be considered as scaling. Using a photocopy machine as an example may help to illustrate. When setting a photocopy machine to make a new image that is smaller than the original, one sets the machine for a percentage that is less than 1, say 50 percent. In this case, the new image will be 50 percent of, or $\frac{1}{2}$ the size of, the original. If one wants an image that is larger than the original, the machine must be set to a percentage that is greater than 1. If the scale factor is set to a multiple of 100—for example, 300 percent—the new image will be three times that of the original. If the scale factor is greater than 1 but not a multiple of 100—for example, 250 percent—the new image will be $2\frac{1}{2}$ times the original.

When we understand the idea of scaling, we can use it to estimate products before performing any actual calculations. If presented with the problem 4×3, for example, we know the product will be greater than 4 because we're scaling up our original value of 4 three times. If we're working on the problem of $4 \times \frac{1}{3}$, we know that our product will be less than 4 because we're scaling down our original value by $\frac{1}{3}$.

n fall 2011, I gave the following problem to 132 students in grades 4, 5, and 6:

Without computing the exact answer, decide which of these expressions would produce the answer with the least value and the greatest value.

A. Addition $\quad\quad \frac{3}{4} + \frac{5}{8}$

B. Subtraction $\quad \frac{3}{4} - \frac{5}{8}$

C. Multiplication $\quad \frac{3}{4} \times \frac{5}{8}$

D. Division $\quad\quad \frac{3}{4} \div \frac{5}{8}$

Not surprisingly, 81 percent of the students chose multiplication as the operation that would result in the answer with the greatest value; 61 percent chose subtraction and 30 percent chose division as the operation that would result in the answer with the least value. Although these answers are incorrect given the numbers and operations involved, they make complete sense in light of students' prior experiences. Generalizations such "Multiplication makes things bigger," and "You can't subtract a smaller number from a larger number" are rooted in students' work with positive integers and serve them fairly well *under specified circumstances*. However, relying on simplifications such as these harms students in the long run, as they approach mathematics as a set of rules to follow instead of relationships to be determined.

6.1 Multiplication Patterns

Materials

Overview

During this activity, students consider patterns of products in problems with factors that decrease in value.

VIDEO CLIP 6a

Introducing Activity 6.1: Multiplication Patterns

In this clip, we see Ms. Lee introducing Activity 6.1 to her fourth graders. Before addressing multiplication with fractions, the activity begins with students solving multiplication problems involving whole numbers. How might starting with whole number multiplication help students solve fraction multiplication problems?

To view this video clip, scan the QR code or access via http://hein.pub/MathOLR

For commentary on the above, see the Appendix: Author's Video Reflections.

1. Display a simple multiplication problem such as *6 × 8* and ask students to name the product.

2. Next, display the problem *6 × 4* and ask students to name the product. Ask students what they notice about the second factor in each problem and the product. Students may first notice that 4 is less than 8 and 24 is less than 48. If no one mentions it, help students to see that the second factor and the product have both diminished by $\frac{1}{2}$: 4 is $\frac{1}{2}$ of 8 and 24 is $\frac{1}{2}$ of 48.

VIDEO CLIP 6b

Noticing Patterns in Factors and Products

In this clip, we hear Denise sharing what she noticed about the factors and products in the problems $6 \times 8 = 48$ and $6 \times 4 = 24$. How do Denise's observations prepare the other students to consider patterns they will encounter in subsequent problems $(6 \times 2, 6 \times 1, 6 \times \underline{\quad})$?

To view this video clip, scan the QR code or access via http://hein.pub/MathOLR

For commentary on the above, see the Appendix: Author's Video Reflections.

3. Display the problem 6×2 and, again, ask students to name the product. Ask the same questions as in Step 2. Ask students if they think there may be a pattern and, if so, whether anyone can describe it in words.

This illustrates Strategy #9 of the ten essential strategies for supporting fraction sense: *Provide opportunities for students to engage in mathematical discourse and share and discuss their mathematical ideas, even those that may not be fully formed or completely accurate.* To learn more about this strategy, see Chapter 8 of *Beyond Pizzas and Pies: 10 Essential Strategies for Supporting Fraction Sense, Grades 3–5, Second Edition* (McNamara and Shaughnessy 2015).

VIDEO CLIP 6c

Moving from Additive to Multiplicative Language

In this clip, we see Emme sharing the pattern she noticed in the factors and products of the first three problems. How does Ms. Lee's rephrasing of Emme's observation help Emme's understanding?

To view this video clip, scan the QR code or access via http://hein.pub/MathOLR

For commentary on the above, see the Appendix: Author's Video Reflections.

4. Display the problem *6 × 1* and repeat Step 3. If it is not mentioned, remind students of the identity property of multiplication, which states that any number multiplied by 1 is that number.

5. Before moving on, ask several students to describe the pattern the problems illustrate. Students may say something like, "When you multiply two numbers and the second factor gets smaller, the product gets smaller," or "When you multiply two numbers and the second factor decreases by half, the product decreases by half."

6. Display *6 × ___* and ask students what number should go in the blank to follow the pattern. You may need to follow-up by asking, "What number is one-half of one?"

VIDEO CLIP 6d

What Number is $\frac{1}{2}$ of 1?

This clip comes after Ms. Lee has written $6 \times$ ___ on the board and asked students what number they think will go in the blank to continue the pattern. Many students respond to Ms. Lee's question by saying "zero." What does this response indicate about their understanding of $\frac{1}{2}$ as the number that would follow the pattern?

To view this video clip, scan the QR code or access via http://hein.pub/MathOLR

For commentary on the above, see the Appendix: Author's Video Reflections.

7. Display *6 × $\frac{1}{2}$* and ask students to name the product. Make sure to ask students to justify their answer using either the pattern from Steps 1 through 6 or another method. If students use repeated addition as their rationale ($\frac{1}{2} + \frac{1}{2} + \frac{1}{2} + \frac{1}{2} + \frac{1}{2} + \frac{1}{2} = 3$), acknowledge that this is another way to prove that $6 \times \frac{1}{2} = 3$. If no one mentions the pattern, help students see that it can also be used to prove that $6 \times \frac{1}{2} = 3$ because $\frac{1}{2}$ is half of 1.

Multiplication as Repeated Addition

After students have established that the next problem should be $6 \times \frac{1}{2}$, Ms. Lee models how repeated addition can be used to find the product of $6 \times \frac{1}{2}$. How might Ms. Lee's modeling here help students?

To view this video clip, scan the QR code or access via http://hein.pub/MathOLR

For commentary on the above, see the Appendix: Author's Video Reflections.

8. Repeat Steps 1 through 7 using another problem, such as

4 × 4

4 × 2

4 × 1

$4 \times \frac{1}{2}$

$4 \times \frac{1}{4}$

6 × 9

6 × 3

6 × 1

$6 \times \frac{1}{3}$, or

7 × 8

7 × 4

7 × 2

7 × 1

$7 \times \frac{1}{2}$

Multiplication with Cuisenaire Rods

Overview

In this activity, students use number lines and Cuisenaire rods to explore the commutative property of multiplication.

Materials

two-unit number lines (**Reproducibles A–B**), 1 per pair of students

Cuisenaire rods, 1 set per pair of students

Manipulative Note

Cuisenaire rods are wooden or plastic blocks that range in length from 1 to 10 cm. Each rod of a given length is the same color. That is, all the 1-cm rods are white, all the 2-cm rods are red, all the 3-cm rods are light green, and so on.

Interpreting $a \times b$

There is some controversy over the interpretation of a multiplication expression such as $a \times b$. Some believe it *must* be interpreted as "a groups of b," whereas others feel it could also be interpreted as "b groups of a." Without a context, either interpretation can be viewed as correct.

1. Provide students with the two-unit number lines and instruct them to cut on the dotted line and tape the pages together to create two-unit number lines. (See Figure 6–14; also available as Reproducibles A and B.)

2. Display the problem $\frac{1}{2} \times 2$. Ask students what the problem means. If students find it difficult to explain the problem, ask them how they would explain the problem if it was 4×2, instead of $\frac{1}{2} \times 2$. Help students to understand that, just as 4×2 can be interpreted to mean four groups of 2 or two groups of 4, $\frac{1}{2} \times 2$ can be interpreted to mean $\frac{1}{2}$ of a group of 2 or two groups of $\frac{1}{2}$.

3. Tell students they will use their Cuisenaire rods and first solve the problem by interpreting it as two groups of $\frac{1}{2}$.

This illustrates Strategy #10 of the ten essential strategies for supporting fraction sense: *Provide opportunities for students to build on their reasoning and sense-making skills about fractions by working with a variety of manipulatives and tools, such as Cuisenaire rods, Pattern Blocks, Fraction Kits, and ordinary items from their lives.* To learn more about this strategy, see Chapters 1, 3, and 4 of Beyond Pizzas & Pies: 10 Essential Strategies for Supporting Fraction Sense, Grades 3–5, Second Edition (McNamara and Shaughnessy 2015).

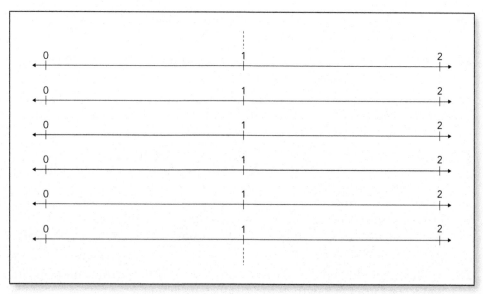

Figure 6–14. Two-Unit Number Lines (Reproducibles A and B, combined)

4. If students are unsure how to begin, ask them to find the rod that equals $\frac{1}{2}$. Students may need a reminder that the referent is the unit interval—for example, the distance from 0 to 1, not the multiunit distance from 0 to 2, so the rod that is $\frac{1}{2}$ of the unit interval is the dark-green rod.

5. Students should find that $2 \times \frac{1}{2} = 1$, as shown here:

6. Encourage students to explain how the rods show that $2 \times \frac{1}{2} = 1$.

7. Next, tell students they will now solve the problem by interpreting it as $\frac{1}{2}$ of 2.

8. Students should first find the length 2, then use a strategy to determine the distance that is $\frac{1}{2}$ the length. Because there is no rod that equals the unit interval, or the length of 1, students have to use another strategy, such as putting two dark-green rods (or two halves) together to find the distance that is half the length of the multi-unit interval of 2.

This illustrates Strategy #7 of the ten essential strategies for supporting fraction sense: *Provide opportunities for students to translate between different fraction representations.* To learn more about this strategy, see Chapter 7 of *Beyond Pizzas & Pies: 10 Essential Strategies for Supporting Fraction Sense, Grades 3–5, Second Edition* (McNamara and Shaughnessy 2015).

9. As before, encourage students to explain how they used the rods or other materials to show that $\frac{1}{2} \times 2 = 1$.

10. Display the problem $\frac{2}{3} \times \frac{1}{2}$. Ask students to interpret the problem. They should tell you that it can either be interpreted to mean $\frac{2}{3}$ *of* $\frac{1}{2}$ or $\frac{1}{2}$ *of* $\frac{2}{3}$.

11. Instruct students to use the rods and the number lines to determine the answer. Make sure you allow sufficient time for students to grapple with the problem before intervening.

12. Students may find they have a much easier time using the rods to solve $\frac{1}{2}$ of $\frac{2}{3}$ than $\frac{2}{3}$ of $\frac{1}{2}$. If this is the case, ask how they would determine the answer to $\frac{1}{3}$ of $\frac{1}{2}$? Encourage students to find a rod that is equal to $\frac{1}{3}$ of $\frac{1}{2}$ using the principles established in Chapter 1, Making Sense: Fractions as Numbers for determining and naming unit fractions.

—————————————————

See also Chapter I, Making Sense: Fractions as Numbers.

—————————————————

13. Students should find that the red rod is $\frac{1}{3}$ of $\frac{1}{2}$, because three of them laid end-to-end are the length of the distance from 0 to $\frac{1}{2}$.

14. After students have determined that $\frac{1}{6}$ is $\frac{1}{3}$ of $\frac{1}{2}$, ask them how they can use that information to find what is $\frac{2}{3}$ of $\frac{1}{2}$.

15. Present the following problems and have students solve them using the two-unit number lines and Cuisenaire rods (make sure students continue to draw on the definition of a unit fraction as established in Chapter 1, Making Sense: Fractions as Numbers):

$4 \times \frac{5}{6}$

$1\frac{1}{2} \times \frac{1}{3}$

$\frac{7}{12} \times 2$

$\frac{1}{6} \times 2\frac{1}{2}$

$\frac{3}{4} \times 3$

$\frac{1}{4} \times \frac{2}{3}$

6.3 Tell Me All You Can, Multiplication

Materials

Overview

This activity (adapted from Bresser and Holzman [2006]) can be used in any content area and is especially helpful when addressing content or concepts that may look somewhat new to students. Students are shown a problem, such as $6 \times 2\frac{1}{2}$, and are told to look closely at the numbers and operations involved. Before coming up with an exact answer, students are to consider and discuss everything they know about the problem as a means of getting a sense of the "neighborhood" of the answer. Problems can be chosen to highlight specific strategies, such as estimation and the use of benchmarks, as well as to bring to light common challenges and misconceptions students often have.

1. Begin by displaying the problem $6 \times 2\frac{1}{2}$ and tell students you don't want them to give you an exact answer, but instead to "tell you all they can" about the answer. If students have trouble coming up with ideas, the following sentence frames may help them get started:

   - The answer will be more than _____ because _____.

     (*The answer will be more than 12 because $6 \times 2 = 12$, and $2\frac{1}{2}$ is more than 2.*)

   - The answer will be less than _____ because _____.

     (*The answer will be less than 18 because $6 \times 3 = 18$, and $2\frac{1}{2}$ is less than 3.*)

   - The answer will be between _____ and _____ because _____.

     (*The answer will be between 12 and 18, because $2\frac{1}{2}$ is more than 2 and less than 3.*)

This illustrates Strategy #9 of the ten essential strategies for supporting fraction sense: *Provide opportunities for students to engage in mathematical discourse and share and discuss their mathematical ideas, even those that may not be fully formed or completely accurate.* To learn more about this strategy, see Chapter 8 of Beyond Pizzas & Pies: 10 Essential Strategies for Supporting Fraction Sense, Grades 3–5, Second Edition (McNamara and Shaughnessy 2015).

VIDEO CLIP 6f

What Do We Know About $6 \times 2\frac{1}{2}$?

In this clip, we see fourth graders discussing what they know about the answer to $6 \times 2\frac{1}{2}$. How can this type of problem help students develop their understanding of mixed numbers?

To view this video clip, scan the QR code or access via http://hein.pub/MathOLR

For commentary on the above, see the Appendix: Author's Video Reflections.

2. You may also ask students questions such as, "Will the answer be more or less than six? How do you know?" and "Will the answer be more or less than two and one-half? How do you know?"

3. Tell students to turn and talk to their neighbor or elbow partner and share their ideas about the answer.

4. When students have had adequate time to discuss the problem with their partner, ask for volunteers to share an idea (either one they thought of or one they heard from their partner) with the whole class.

VIDEO CLIP 6g

"$6 \times 2\frac{1}{2}$ Has to Be Greater Than $2\frac{1}{2}$"

In this clip, we see Lizette stating that the answer to $6 \times 2\frac{1}{2}$ has to be greater than $2\frac{1}{2}$. What important mathematical property is Lizette drawing on with this statement?

To view this video clip, scan the QR code or access via http://hein.pub/MathOLR

For commentary on the above, see the Appendix: Author's Video Reflections.

VIDEO CLIP 6h

Applying the Distributive Property to Reason About the Product of $6 \times 2\frac{1}{2}$

In this clip, we see two students sharing what they know about the answer to $6 \times 2\frac{1}{2}$. What do the students' responses indicate that they understand about multiplication and the distributive property?

To view this video clip, scan the QR code or access via http://hein.pub/MathOLR

For commentary on the above, see the Appendix: Author's Video Reflections.

5. Chart students' contributions, and be sure to ask students for their rationale if they do not provide it without prompting.

6. Display another problem and repeat the process.

VIDEO CLIP 6i

$4\frac{1}{2}$ Is More Than 4 But Less Than 5

In this clip, Gregorio shares how he knows that $4\frac{1}{2} \times 5$ will be more than 20 and another student agrees with his reasoning. Why does Ms. McNamara ask Dat to share his rationale for thinking that $4\frac{1}{2} \times 5$ is less than 25?

To view this video clip, scan the QR code or access via http://hein.pub/MathOLR

For commentary on the above, see the Appendix: Author's Video Reflections.

Making Estimates

Materials
none

Overview

During this activity (which has been adapted from Burns [2003]), students estimate answers to problems that involve multiplying fractions, mixed numbers, and whole numbers.

1. Display the problem $6 \times 2\frac{1}{2}$ and ask students to think on their own first to come up with an estimate for the answer.

2. After students have decided on an estimate, have them share their estimates with a partner and explain their rationale. Allow students to change their estimate in response to this sharing if they desire.

3. Ask for volunteers to tell you their estimates and display them in order of magnitude, writing the estimates with the least value to the left and the greatest value to the right as shown here:

$$6 \times 2\frac{1}{2}$$

Estimates:

12	$12\frac{1}{2}$	15	$16\frac{1}{3}$	18	21

4. After all estimates have been displayed, ask students to identify any that can be eliminated. In the example shown, 12 can be eliminated because the answer must be greater than 12, because $6 \times 2 = 12$, and $2\frac{1}{2}$ is greater than 2.

5. After students have identified all the estimates that can be eliminated, tell them they will repeat the process with five other problems. After they have narrowed down the estimates, they will have a chance to determine the exact answer to one of the problems.

This illustrates Strategy #9 of the ten essential strategies for supporting fraction sense: *Provide opportunities for students to engage in mathematical discourse and share and discuss their mathematical ideas, even those that may not be fully formed or completely accurate.* To learn more about this strategy, see Chapter 8 of *Beyond Pizzas & Pies: 10 Essential Strategies for Supporting Fraction Sense, Grades 3–5, Second Edition* (McNamara and Shaughnessy 2015).

6. Display the following problems, one at a time, and repeat Steps 1 through 4:

$4\frac{1}{2} \times 2\frac{3}{4}$

$3\frac{1}{2} \times \frac{2}{3}$

$4 \times \frac{3}{4}$

$7\frac{1}{2} \times 2\frac{1}{3}$

$3\frac{3}{4} \times 7$

Differentiation Strategy

Allowing students to choose the problem they will solve is a great way to differentiate instruction.

7. This next step may be a homework assignment or you may choose to present it to students the next day. Tell students they are to select one of the problems that was discussed and find an exact answer. They should be prepared to share their solution and strategy with their classmates.

6.5 Paper Folding

Materials
5 × 5-inch squares of paper, several for each student
colored pencils, 1 set per group of 4

Overview

Students fold paper squares to represent the multiplication algorithm and to provide a visual model that shows why multiplication doesn't always make things bigger. In addition, the importance of identifying the whole is emphasized.

1. Remind students of how they have used an area model in the past to represent multiplication of whole numbers. You may want to display an example such as the one shown here, to represent *5 × 4*.

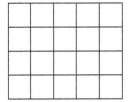

2. Tell students that an area model can also be used to represent multiplication of fractions.

3. Pass out the paper squares. Tell students that the square represents a farmer's field.

Field

4. Tell students that the farmer wants to plant $\frac{1}{2}$ her field with fruit and the other $\frac{1}{2}$ with vegetables. Show them how to fold the paper carefully in half vertically and use one color to lightly shade and label one of the halves to show the part of the field that will be planted with fruit. Then, use another color to shade and label the other half to show the part of the field that will be planted with vegetables.

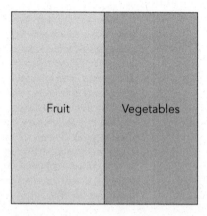

5. Make sure that students are in agreement that the "field" is now equally partitioned so that $\frac{1}{2}$ of the field is for fruit and $\frac{1}{2}$ of the field is for vegetables.

6. Next, tell students the farmer wants to partition the two halves of her field in the following ways: $\frac{1}{2}$ of the fruit section will be planted with fruit trees and $\frac{1}{2}$ with fruit bushes. Half of the vegetable section will be planted with vegetables that grow above ground and half with vegetables that grow below ground.

7. Instruct students to fold the paper in half horizontally so they create four equal sections. As before, have them lightly shade and label each section.

Fruit Trees	Above-Ground Vegetables
Fruit Bushes	Below-Ground Vegetables

8. Ask students to identify what fraction of the farmer's field is planted with fruit trees, what fraction is planted with fruit bushes, what fraction is planted with above-ground vegetables, and what fraction is planted with below-ground vegetables. Make sure to ask students to provide justification for their responses.

9. Pose the following problem to students and ask them to discuss with a partner or small group:

How does the "field" show that $\frac{1}{2} \times \frac{1}{2} = \frac{1}{4}$?

Fruit Trees	Above-Ground Vegetables
Fruit Bushes	Below-Ground Vegetables

This illustrates Strategy #10 of the ten essential strategies for supporting fraction sense: *Provide opportunities for students to build on their reasoning and sense-making skills about fractions by working with a variety of manipulatives and tools, such as Cuisenaire rods, Pattern Blocks, Fraction Kits, and ordinary items from their lives.* To learn more about this strategy, see Chapters 1, 3, and 4 of *Beyond Pizzas & Pies: 10 Essential Strategies for Supporting Fraction Sense, Grades 3–5, Second Edition* (McNamara and Shaughnessy 2015).

10. After students have had sufficient time to discuss with a partner or small group, bring them together and ask for volunteers to share their thinking or a classmate's thinking. To reinforce the importance of identifying the whole, be sure to emphasize that when the whole is the part of the field planted with fruit, the correct answer to the question, "What fraction is planted with fruit trees?" is "one-half." However, when the whole is the entire field, the correct answer to the question, "What fraction is planted with fruit trees?" is "one fourth." In addition, to support students' understanding of the multiplication algorithm, ask questions such as, "Why is the denominator of the product four?" and "Why is the product smaller than either of the numbers being multiplied?"

11. Hand out another paper square and present the following scenario:

- Another farmer is going to plant $\frac{1}{2}$ of his field with flowers and leave the other $\frac{1}{2}$ unplanted to use as a pasture.
- He plans to use $\frac{1}{3}$ of the flower half for roses, $\frac{1}{3}$ for daisies, and $\frac{1}{3}$ for geraniums.
- What fraction of the field will be planted with roses?
- What fraction of the field will be planted with daisies?
- What fraction of the field will be planted with geraniums?

12. Allow time for students to make sense of the problem and decide how to use the paper to solve it. If they are unsure how to proceed, encourage them to consider how the paper helped them find the answers to the previous problem.

13. After students have had sufficient time to find their answer, ask for volunteers to share their thinking or a classmate's thinking.

14. As the discussion is winding down, present the following problem to the students:

If the farmer decided that he really didn't like geraniums and instead planted $\frac{2}{3}$ of the flower section with daisies and kept $\frac{1}{3}$ for roses, how much of the field would be planted with daisies?

15. Allow time for students to talk with a partner or small group about the answer, and ask for volunteers to share their thinking or a classmate's thinking.

16. If time allows, the following is an additional problem for students to solve using the paper-folding strategy:

A school playground is $\frac{1}{3}$ concrete, $\frac{1}{3}$ grass, and $\frac{1}{3}$ dirt. Three-fourths of the dirt section is going to be used as a garden. What fraction of the entire playground will be used for the garden?

17. As before, allow time for students to talk with a partner or small group about the answer, then ask for volunteers to share their thinking or a classmate's thinking.

Teaching Tip

Students may have difficulty folding the paper accurately into thirds. Although it can be tempting to present them with a strategy for doing so, allowing them to work through this challenge can provide a meaningful context to reinforce the meaning of $\frac{1}{3}$.

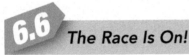

6.6 | **The Race Is On!**

Materials
The Race Is On!, recording sheet (**Reproducible 6a**), 1 per student

Overview

The context of a relay race is used to help students explore the inverse relationship between multiplication and division.

1. Tell students they are going to solve a series of problems about students running a relay race.

2. Pass out *The Race Is On!* recording sheet, one to each student. (See Figure 6–15; also available as Reproducible 6a.)

3. Ask a volunteer to read the description of the problem at the top of the page.

4. When you are sure students understand the context, ask for suggested answers to the first question: *If Max and Mila don't find any friends to join them, how far will they each need to travel?*

5. If students suggest more than one answer, you may choose to write all suggestions on the board first, then ask for volunteers to defend one of the answers. This can be an effective way of encouraging all students to share their thinking, and can also be an instructive and nonthreatening way to narrow down the suggestions to a correct answer.

6. Make sure students understand the problem can be solved using either multiplication ($\frac{1}{2} \times 15$ or $15 \times \frac{1}{2}$) or division ($15 \div 2$).

REPRODUCIBLE 6A

The Race Is On!

Date: _____

Name: _____

Waterside School is holding a 15-mile relay race to raise money for a new library. Teams can consist of up to 30 people, as long as each participant on a team runs or walks the same distance. Mila and Max decide to make a team.

1. If Max and Mila don't find any friends to join them, how far will they each need to travel?

2. If Max's younger sister Marva decides to join the team, how far will they each need to travel?

3. Mila's cousin also decides to join the team. How far will each teammate need to travel now?

4. Max and Mila's team is getting very popular so they decide to create a chart to show how far each person on a team must travel for teams of any size, from 1 person to 30 people. Work with your group to complete a similar chart.

Figure 6–15. *The Race Is On!*, recording sheet

Understanding the Context

Students may not be familiar with the context of a relay race. Make sure they understand that the total distance traveled is 15 miles. How far each person runs depends on how many people are on the team.

7. When students have agreed that Max and Mila each need to travel 7 $\frac{1}{2}$ miles, ask a volunteer to read Question 2: *If Max's younger sister Marva decides to join the team, how far will they each need to travel?*

8. Again, ask for suggested answers with explanations. Also, ask students to identify how the problem can be solved using either multiplication ($\frac{1}{3} \times 15$ or $15 \times \frac{1}{3}$) or division ($15 \div 3$).

> ### Teaching Tip
>
> You may choose to solve Question 3 with the whole class or allow students to begin working on the group task after discussing Question 2.

9. Tell students that they will continue to work on *The Race Is On!* and create a chart as described in Question 4: *Max and Mila's team is getting very popular so they decide to create a chart to show how far each person on a team must travel for teams of any size, from 1 person to 30 people. Work with your group to complete a similar chart.* Depending on your students, you may want to suggest how they can split up the task as well as how to record their findings.

10. After students have completed their charts, have them compare their results. Ask which of the team sizes were easiest to solve (5, 15, or 30) and which were more challenging. Choose a few to go over with the whole group, making sure students explain their strategies and identify how the problems could be solved with either multiplication or division.

Helping students connect what they know about whole-number multiplication to multiplying with fractions is essential. Encouraging them to identify patterns, estimate products, defend their answers, and explore the relationship between multiplication and division is necessary for making this connection.

Study Questions

After Reading Chapter 6

1. What information presented in the "Classroom Scenario," "What's the Math?," and "What's the Research?" sections was familiar to you or similar to your experience with students?

2. Using one's knowledge of whole number multiplication to understand fraction multiplication is a somewhat different approach to multiplying fractions than we have seen in the past. How will this change influence how you approach fraction multiplication with your students?

3. Which of the Classroom Activities (Activity 6.1, *Multiplication Patterns*; Activity 6.2, *Multiplication with Cuisenaire Rods*; Activity 6.3, *Tell Me All You Can*, Activity 6.4, *Making Estimates*; Activity 6.5, *Paper Folding*; or Activity 6.6, *The Race Is On!*) do you plan to implement with your students?

After Trying One or More of the Activities

1. Describe the activity and any modifications you made to meet your students' needs or to align with your curriculum.

2. How did this activity add to your knowledge of what your students do and do not understand about multiplying fractions?

3. What are your next steps for supporting your students' learning about multiplying fractions?

Connections with *Beyond Pizzas & Pies, Second Edition*

Beyond Invert & Multiply builds on the foundational understandings introduced in its companion resource, *Beyond Pizzas & Pies, Second Edition*. I recommend pairing this chapter with Chapters 2 and 7 in *Beyond Pizzas & Pies, Second Edition* to continue your learning.

Making Sense
Division with Fractions

O U T L I N E

CCSS Connections

Prerequisite Standards

3.NF.A.1: Understand a fraction $1/b$ as the quantity formed by 1 part when a whole is partitioned into b equal parts; understand a fraction a/b as the quantity formed by a parts of size $1/b$.

3.NF.A.2: Understand a fraction as a number on the number line; represent fractions on a number line diagram.

4.NF.B.3: Understand a fraction a/b with $a > 1$ as a sum of fractions $1/b$.

5.NF.B.3: Interpret a fraction as division of the numerator by the denominator $(a/b = a \div b)$. Solve word problems involving division of whole numbers leading to answers in the form of fractions or mixed numbers.

Standards Addressed

5.NF.B.7: Apply and extend previous understanding of division to divide unit fractions by whole numbers and whole numbers by unit fractions.

6.NS.A.1: Interpret and compute quotients of fractions, and solve word problems involving division of fractions by fractions.

Before beginning his lesson on fraction division Mr. Franz asked students to share what they know about dividing fractions. Most of the sixth graders had heard of the strategy of inverting and multiplying, but no one could give an explanation of why you had to do it, nor why it worked. As the discussion was winding down Sadie raised her hand.

"Yes, Sadie? Do you have something to add?" Mr. Franz asked.

"I don't really understand why you have to invert and multiply. Can't you just divide across the fraction to get the answer?"

Knowing that Sadie often made very good points during class discussions, and not quite sure where she was going with her idea, Mr. Franz invited her up to the board to continue.

"OK," Sadie began, writing $\frac{4}{9} \div \frac{2}{3}$ on the board. "Four divided by two is two and nine divided by three is three, so the answer is two-thirds," Sadie continued as the other students watched skeptically.

$$\frac{4}{9} \div \frac{2}{3} = \frac{2}{3}$$

"See, you get the same answer if you do it the other way," Sadie added as she wrote $\frac{4}{9} \times \frac{3}{2} = \frac{12}{18} = \frac{2}{3}$ on the board.

"Wait a minute!" "Whoa! That's awesome!" "What the heck?!" several other students exclaimed.

"Hmm, let's try another example and see if it works with that one," Mr. Franz suggested.

"I knew you'd say that, Mr. F, so I'm all ready for you!" Sadie said, grinning, as she wrote $\frac{15}{8} \div \frac{3}{4}$ on the board. "This one works, too. Go ahead. Try it," Sadie encouraged her classmates.

$$\frac{15}{8} \div \frac{3}{4} = \frac{5}{2}$$

"OMG, Sadie! You're a genius! It does work," Richie said, excitedly. "Mr. F, why didn't you just teach us to do that?"

Sensing a possible rebellion, Mr. Franz considered presenting an example that didn't work out quite so nicely. His thought process was interrupted by Shen.

"Uh oh," Shen called out. "It doesn't always work. Can I come up?" he asked, looking back and forth between Sadie and Mr. Franz.

Without waiting for a response, Shen came to the front of the room and wrote $\frac{3}{4} \div \frac{2}{3}$ on the board. He then tried to solve it using Sadie's method, which resulted in the quotient $\dfrac{\frac{3}{2}}{\frac{4}{3}}$. He then simplified the numerator and denominator to arrive at $\dfrac{1\frac{1}{2}}{1\frac{1}{3}}$.

$$\frac{3}{4} \div \frac{2}{3} = \frac{\frac{3}{2}}{\frac{4}{3}} = \frac{1\frac{1}{2}}{1\frac{1}{3}}$$

"I have no idea what to call that!" Shen gestured dramatically. "Mr. F, can you even have a fraction over a fraction? I mean, is that even legit?"

Mr. Franz looked around the class to do a quick assessment of their interest level. He knew he could count on Sadie, Shen, and a few other students who would happily pursue this line of reasoning, but he needed to make sure it would be fruitful for the rest of his sixth graders. Based on the genuinely interested and enthusiastic looks on their faces, he decided to continue.

"I agree with Shen, and the rest of you, that it looks pretty strange to have a fraction over a fraction. When you have a fraction with a fraction in either the numerator, denominator, or both, it's called a *complex fraction*. We haven't seen complex fractions before, but you will likely see them again in high school," Mr. Franz explained.

Mr. Franz thought for a moment about how to proceed. He knew that most students would be able to determine that Sadie's method "worked" because of the relationship between the numerators and denominators in the fractions she had chosen. He was less sure, however, that many students would come to the conclusion that Sadie's method also worked with Shen's fractions, and that his answer with the complex fraction was actually equivalent to $\frac{9}{8}$, the answer one arrives at when using the traditional invert-and-multiply strategy.

Deciding to tackle Sadie's strategy first, Mr. Franz wrote the following problems on the board and asked the class to determine which ones worked with Sadie's method and which ones didn't. He knew that arriving at a complex fraction would be enough to convince many students that Sadie's method only worked sometimes. He hoped that by allowing time for the students to muck around with the mathematics, they would come to the realization that Sadie's method always worked, just more elegantly and efficiently in some cases than in others.

$$\frac{8}{15} \div \frac{4}{5}$$

$$\frac{4}{9} \div \frac{3}{2}$$

$$\frac{2}{3} \div \frac{5}{6}$$

$$\frac{10}{21} \div \frac{5}{7}$$

After agreeing that Sadie's method worked with $\frac{8}{15} \div \frac{4}{5}$ and $\frac{10}{21} \div \frac{5}{7}$, but not $\frac{4}{9} \div \frac{3}{2}$ and $\frac{2}{3} \div \frac{5}{6}$, Mr. Franz told the students to discuss *why* Sadie's method worked with some problems but not with others.

As the students were discussing the problems, Mr. Franz circulated and listened in on the conversations at the students' tables. He was pleased to hear that many of the conversations focused on generalizations about the relationships between the numerators and denominators in the problems, and that students were using appropriate mathematical language when sharing their generalizations.

As he called the students back together, Mr. Franz asked Table 4 to share a bit of their conversation with the class.

"Table four, you had an interesting way of talking about the problems that worked and didn't work. Would you mind sharing that with the class?"

"Sure," began Natalie, who often served as spokesperson for her group. "We decided to replace the numbers with letters, so instead of eight-fifteenths divided by four-fifths, for example, we have a over b divided by c over d. Then, when we looked at the problems that work, we noticed that if a is a multiple of c—"

"Or c is a factor of a," Arun interrupted.

"Yeah, or c is a factor of a," Natalie added, agreeing with Arun, "and b is a multiple of d—or d is a factor of b—then Sadie's method works."

"And if you don't have that relationship," Arun continued, "then Sadie's method doesn't exactly work."

"What do you mean by 'Sadie's method doesn't exactly work?'" Mr. Franz asked, knowing there had been disagreement at this table about what students meant by the method "working."

"Well," Arun replied, pointing to the problem Shen had written on the board "in the problem that Shen shared, three-fourths divided by two-thirds, the answer that you get when you use Sadie's method is three-halves over four-thirds, which simplifies to one and one-half over one and one-third. And if you do it the invert and multiply way," he continued, coming up to the front of the room and writing $\frac{3}{4} \times \frac{3}{2}$ on the board, "you get nine-eighths, which simplifies to one and one-eighth. And I have a feeling that one and one-half over one and one-third is the same as one and one-eighth."

$$\frac{3}{4} \div \frac{2}{3} = \frac{\frac{3}{2}}{\frac{4}{3}} = \frac{1\frac{1}{2}}{1\frac{1}{3}} \qquad\qquad \frac{3}{4} \times \frac{3}{2} = \frac{9}{8} = 1\frac{1}{8}$$

As Arun returned to his seat, Mr. Franz looked around the class to see if anyone else was following his thinking. Feeling the tension between honoring Arun's interest in continuing to wrestle with the problem and keeping the rest of his students focused and engaged, Mr. Franz decided to table the discussion and return to it after the series of lessons he had planned on fraction division. He asked Arun to add his question "Is one and one-half over one and one-third the same as one and one-eighth?" to the "parking lot" posted on a wall of the classroom and suggested that interested students could investigate this question when they had free time. He knew that Arun and a handful of other students would really enjoy digging into this problem, and Mr. Franz looked forward to discussing it with them further. For the rest of the period, however, he went back to his original lesson plan and asked students to think of a context that could be represented by the problem *6 ÷ 2*.

Sadie's Method

In the classroom scenario, Sadie discovers something that may come as a surprise to many of us. In many cases, one can divide fractions *without* using the invert and multiply method. As the students in the scenario discovered, Sadie's method works when the numerator and denominator of the dividend are multiples of the numerator and denominator of the divisor, respectively. Given the first example that Sadie presented, $\frac{4}{9} \div \frac{2}{3}$, our quotient is easily acquired by dividing across the numerators ($4 \div 2 = 2$) and denominators ($9 \div 3 = 3$).

$$\frac{4}{9} \div \frac{2}{3} = \frac{2}{3}$$

Shen's example of a problem that doesn't work using Sadie's method leads us nicely to one explanation of the invert-and-multiply algorithm. Let's start with Shen's attempt to use Sadie's method to divide $\frac{3}{4}$ by $\frac{2}{3}$. Using Sadie's method we get a complex fraction as our quotient:

STEP 1

$$\frac{3}{4} \div \frac{2}{3} = \frac{\frac{3}{2}}{\frac{4}{3}}$$

To get rid of the fraction in the denominator of the quotient, we can multiply $\frac{4}{3}$ by its multiplicative inverse, $\frac{3}{4}$. Of course, to maintain the value of the fraction, we have to do the same thing to the numerator of the quotient as well:

STEP 2

$$\frac{\frac{3}{2}}{\frac{4}{3}} \times \frac{\frac{3}{4}}{\frac{3}{4}} = \frac{\frac{9}{8}}{\frac{12}{12}}$$

Because $\frac{4}{3} \times \frac{3}{4} = 1$, the denominator of our quotient is now $\frac{12}{12}$ (or 1), and the numerator is $\frac{9}{8}$. We know that, because of the identity property, $\frac{9}{8} \div 1 = \frac{9}{8}$, so we can write the quotient without a denominator. If we look closely at the numerators of our equation, we see the original dividend ($\frac{3}{4}$), the inverse of the original divisor ($\frac{3}{2}$), and our quotient ($\frac{9}{8}$). By using the invert-and-multiply method we have bypassed Steps 1 and 2, and gone directly to Step 3.

STEP 3

$$\frac{3}{2} \times \frac{3}{4} = \frac{9}{8}$$

Of course, we typically write the number in the new equation in the same order as in the original equation. Because we're dealing with multiplication, as a result of the commutative property, the order of the numbers being multiplied doesn't matter:

$$\frac{3}{4} \times \frac{3}{2} = \frac{9}{8}$$

Arun's Wondering

Logically, by going through the previous steps, we can accept that, as Arun said in the classroom scenario, "one and one-half over one and one-third is the same as one and one-eighth," because both answers are the result of dividing $\frac{3}{4}$ by $\frac{2}{3}$. The question remains, however, of how to prove that the two answers are, in fact, equivalent. One way to begin is to consider the problem using a quotitive interpretation (see Chapter 5 for a discussion of quotitive and partitive division). When faced with a quotitive division problem, such as $a \div b = ?$, one can ask, "How many b's are in a?" This is fairly easy to consider when working with whole numbers. Given the problem, $6 \div 2 = ?$, I can ask, "How many twos are in six?" and easily arrive at the quotient, 3. With fractions, this can be a bit more challenging, but can be aided by considering the numbers in a measurement context.

See Chapter 5, Developing Awareness: Multiplication and Division Problem Types.

Let's consider $\frac{3}{4} \div \frac{2}{3}$. Suppose I have $\frac{3}{4}$ of a gallon of paint and I need $\frac{2}{3}$ of a gallon to paint a wall. I want to know how many $\frac{2}{3}$ of a gallon are in $\frac{3}{4}$ of a gallon, or how many walls I can cover with the paint I have. (See Figure 7–1.)

Figure 7–1 shows that, within the $\frac{3}{4}$ of a gallon of paint, there is $\frac{2}{3}$ of a gallon (or enough paint for one wall) and another $\frac{1}{12}$ of a gallon more (shaded dark gray).

By partitioning the original gallon further into twelfths, we can see that $\frac{1}{12}$ of a gallon is one-eighth of $\frac{2}{3}$ of a gallon, because there are eight $\frac{1}{12}$s in $\frac{2}{3}$. (See Figure 7–2.)

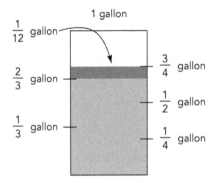

Figure 7–1. How many $\frac{2}{3}$ of a gallon are in $\frac{3}{4}$ of a gallon?

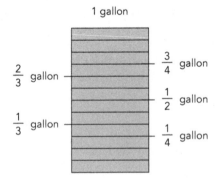

Figure 7–2. One-twelfth of one gallon is $\frac{1}{8}$ of $\frac{2}{3}$ of a gallon.

Shen's Quotient

We can use a similar strategy to make sense of the quotient Shen arrived at when using Sadie's method to solve $\frac{3}{4} \div \frac{2}{3}$. Recall that when dividing directly across numerators and denominators, Shen ended up with one and one-half over one and one-third. If we interpret the fraction bar as indicating division, we can also consider this as $1\frac{1}{2} \div 1\frac{1}{3}$, and can ask, "How many one and one-thirds are in one and one-half?" A number line can help us make sense of this situation:

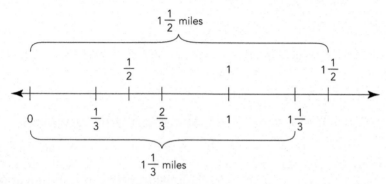

If we imagine a context around a distance, perhaps $1\frac{1}{2}$ miles, and ask, "How many one and one-third miles are in one and one-half miles?" we can show on the number line that there is one length of $1\frac{1}{3}$ miles plus a bit more (see below). By partitioning the number line further, we determine that the bit more is actually $\frac{1}{6}$ of a mile, and because there are eight $\frac{1}{6}$s in $1\frac{1}{3}$, $\frac{1}{6}$ is $\frac{1}{8}$ of $1\frac{1}{3}$.

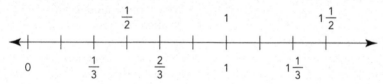

Finding Common Denominators Before Dividing

Another strategy for fraction division that avoids the need to invert and multiply involves renaming the dividend and divisor to fractions with common denominators. Returning to Shen's problem, $\frac{3}{4} \div \frac{2}{3}$, we rename $\frac{3}{4}$ as $\frac{9}{12}$ and $\frac{2}{3}$ as $\frac{8}{12}$. Now our problem is $\frac{9}{12} \div \frac{8}{12}$:

$$\left(\frac{3}{4} \times \frac{3}{3}\right) \div \left(\frac{2}{3} \times \frac{4}{4}\right) = \frac{9}{12} \div \frac{8}{12}$$

$$\frac{9}{12} \div \frac{8}{12} = \frac{\frac{9}{8}}{\frac{12}{12}}$$

Twelve divided by twelve is one, so we can disregard the denominator in the quotient and we are once again left with $\frac{9}{8}$.

Connection Between Multiplication and Division

To help us understand why we get the same result when we transform a division problem by inverting the divisor and multiplying, we need to understand the relationship between multiplication and division. Multiplication and division are *inverse operations*—meaning, you can use one to undo the other. When a number is multiplied by its *multiplicative inverse*, the resulting product is 1. For example, $\frac{1}{6}$ is the multiplicative inverse of 6 (and 6 is the multiplicative inverse of $\frac{1}{6}$) because, when multiplied together, the product is 1, which is the identity element for multiplication. We can talk about this in general terms by saying $a \times \frac{1}{a} = 1$.

> **Multiplication and division are *inverse operations*—meaning, you can use one to undo the other.**

We also know that any number divided by itself also equals 1, or to use our previous example, $a \div a = 1$. When we compare these two equations, we see something interesting:

$$a \times \frac{1}{a} = 1$$

$$a \div a = 1$$

Multiplying by $\frac{1}{a}$ and dividing by a get us to the same result: 1. From here, we can generalize to say that multiplying by a number and dividing by its inverse are mathematically equivalent. A real-world example with a whole-number dividend can help to illustrate.

Assume you have 28 students in your class and you want to split them into two equal groups. There are two equations you can use to arrive at the answer of 14. The first way is to consider $28 \div 2$; you have 28 students and you need to put them into two equal groups. The second way is to consider $28 \times \frac{1}{2}$ or, more likely, $\frac{1}{2} \times 28$, in which case you need to determine how many students make up half of the class of 28. Most of us have little problem understanding how

$28 \div 2$ and $28 \times \frac{1}{2}$ are the same mathematically. We can use the same logic with a problem with a fraction as the dividend.

Imagine you have a cookie recipe that calls for a half of a cup sugar. You decide to make half of a batch of cookies so you need to figure out how much sugar to use. One way to think about it is to use the expression $\frac{1}{2} \div 2$, and then determine how much sugar you would have if you divided your $\frac{1}{2}$ cup into two equal portions. Another way to think about it is with the expression $\frac{1}{2} \times \frac{1}{2}$, in which you would ask, "What is one-half of one-half cup?" Both expressions, $\frac{1}{2} \div 2$ and $\frac{1}{2} \times \frac{1}{2}$, net you the same result: $\frac{1}{4}$ cup.

Doing the Same Thing to the Dividend and Divisor

Let's look at inverting and multiplying in another way. Let's consider what happens to the quotient in a division problem when the dividend and divisor are multiplied or divided by the same number. Again, an example using whole numbers will get us started.

Solve the following problems and come up with a generalization about the effect on the quotient:

$$12 \div 6$$

$$(12 \times 4) \div (6 \times 4)$$

$$(12 \div 2) \div (6 \div 2)$$

$$(12 \times 5) \div (6 \times 5)$$

$$(12 \div 3) \div (6 \div 3)$$

In every example, the quotient is 2. It is pretty clear that multiplying or dividing the dividend and the divisor *by the same number* does not affect the quotient. You may be thinking "OK, but what does that have to do with dividing fractions?" Given Shen's problem, $\frac{3}{4} \div \frac{2}{3}$, we can use the same strategy (multiplying the dividend and divisor by the same number) and avoid the pesky complex fraction. We start with Shen's original problem:

$$\frac{3}{4} \div \frac{2}{3}$$

Then, we multiply the dividend and divisor by $\frac{3}{2}$ (the multiplicative inverse of $\frac{2}{3}$):

$$\left(\frac{3}{4} \times \frac{3}{2}\right) \div \left(\frac{2}{3} \times \frac{3}{2}\right)$$

Because $\frac{2}{3} \times \frac{3}{2} = 1$, our expression now reads:

$$\left(\frac{3}{4} \times \frac{3}{2}\right) \div 1$$

Because any number divided by 1 equals that number, we can disregard the division by 1 and we are left with:

$$\left(\frac{3}{4} \times \frac{3}{2}\right)$$

Tirosh states in a study published in 2000 that, "Division of fractions is often considered the most mechanical and least understood topic in elementary school," and that the types of mistakes children make when dividing fractions fall into three main categories. Tirosh (2000, 6) identifies the first of these as "algorithmically based mistakes," or mistakes that stem from forgetting or changing the steps of the algorithm, such as inverting the dividend instead of the divisor. The second type of mistake is referred to as "intuitively based mistakes," which are often the result of overgeneralizing properties of operations based on previous experience with division of natural numbers. The third type of mistake is "mistakes based on formal knowledge," such as mistakes based on the assumption that division, like multiplication, is commutative.

In response to Tirosh's findings, Newton and Sands (2012) report a series of lessons aimed at helping sixth-grade students make sense of fraction division. After reviewing fraction multiplication, students were guided to the following generalization about fraction multiplication:

$$\frac{a}{b} \times \frac{c}{d} = \frac{ac}{bd}$$

Students then solved a series of division problems that could be solved by dividing across numerators and denominators, as shown here:

$$\frac{8}{21} \div \frac{2}{3} = \frac{4}{7}$$

Not surprisingly, the students were in agreement that dividing across numerators and denominators was a reasonable method for finding the quotient.

The students' teacher then followed up with a problem that didn't work quite so nicely with the dividing-across method: $\frac{3}{5} \div \frac{1}{2}$. Two strategies emerged for solving this problem. The first was to rename the dividend as $\frac{6}{10}$, thus transforming the problem to one that was quite easily solved using the divide-across method:

$$\frac{6}{10} \div \frac{1}{2} = \frac{6}{5}$$

The second method involved dividing across numerators and denominators, and then multiplying the quotient by $\frac{2}{2}$ to address the issue of the fraction in the denominator:

$$\frac{3}{5} \div \frac{1}{2} = \frac{3}{2\frac{1}{2}} \times \frac{2}{2} = \frac{6}{5}$$

After solving other similar problems (in other words, problems that resulted in a fraction in the denominator of the quotient), the students determined that the divide-across method worked well in some situations but was somewhat unwieldy in others. To provide students with a method that would work in all cases, students compared equivalent multiplication and division problems such as $4 \times \frac{1}{4}$ and $4 \div 4$, and found that "dividing by a number was equivalent to multiplying by that number's reciprocal" (Newton and Sands 2012, 344).

After the series of lessons, students were presented with several problems, some of which could be solved easily using the divide-across method and others that were solved more easily using the standard algorithm. Although some students chose to use the standard algorithm for both types of problems, several students selected their strategy appropriately based on the numbers involved in the problems. This type of decision making on the part of students, as opposed to blindly using an algorithm with little understanding, is a great way to support students to make sense of mathematical situations and to decrease the likelihood of the types of mistakes discussed at the beginning of this section.

7.1 Division Patterns

Materials

Overview

During this activity, students consider patterns of quotients in problems with divisors that decrease in value.

1. Display a simple division problem such as $8 \div 8$ and ask students to name the quotient.

2. Next, display the problem $8 \div 4$ and ask students to name the quotient. Ask students what they notice about the divisor in each problem and the quotient. Students may first notice that 4 is less than 8 and 2 is more than 1. If no one mentions it, help students to see that the divisor has diminished by $\frac{1}{2}$ (4 is half of 8), but the quotient has doubled (2 is twice 1).

3. Display the problem $8 \div 2$ and ask students to name the quotient. Ask the same questions as in Step 2. Ask students if they think there may be a pattern and, if so, whether anyone can describe it in words.

4. Display the problem $8 \div 1$ and repeat Step 3. If it is not mentioned, remind students that any number divided by 1 results in a quotient that is the same as the dividend.

5. Before moving on, ask several students to describe the pattern the problems illustrate and encourage them to use the terms, *dividend*, *divisor*, and *quotient*. Students may say something like, "When you divide a number by another number, the answer (or quotient) gets bigger when the divisor gets smaller " or "When you divide a number by another number, the answer (or quotient) gets smaller when the divisor gets larger."

This illustrates Strategy #9 of the ten essential strategies for supporting fraction sense: *Provide opportunities for students to engage in mathematical discourse and share and discuss their mathematical ideas, even those that may not be fully formed or completely accurate.* To learn more about this strategy, see Chapter 8 of *Beyond Pizzas & Pies: 10 Essential Strategies for Supporting Fraction Sense, Grades 3–5*, Second Edition (McNamara and Shaughnessy 2015).

6. Display $8 \div \underline{\hspace{1cm}}$ and ask students what number should go in the blank to follow the pattern. You may need to follow up by asking, "What number is one-half of one?"

7. Display $8 \div \frac{1}{2}$ and ask students to name the quotient. Make sure to ask students to justify their answer using either the pattern from Steps 1 through 6 or another method. If students use a quotitive interpretation of division as their rationale (two $\frac{1}{2}$s make up every 1, so there are sixteen $\frac{1}{2}$s in 8), acknowledge this is another way to prove that $8 \div \frac{1}{2} = 16$. If no one mentions the pattern, help students see that it can also be used to prove that $8 \div \frac{1}{2} = 16$.

8. Repeat Steps 1 through 7 using another problem.

7.2 How Long? How Far?

Materials

two-unit number lines (**Reproducibles A and B**), 1 per pair of students

Cuisenaire rods, 1 set per pair of students

giant Cuisenaire rods or tag board "rods" with magnetic tape for display

stopwatch or some way of timing to the quarter minute

Overview

Students use the contexts of time and distance to solve problems involving division of whole numbers by a fraction and division of a fraction by a whole number. The contexts help students connect what they know about division with whole numbers to division with fractions. This lesson may take place over two or more class periods.

Part I

1. Explain to students that they are going to learn about dividing fractions. Ask them what they know about division. If a student says something like, "Division makes things smaller," let this statement stay out there because you'll return to it at the end of the lesson. Record students' statements so you can come back to them at the end of the activity.

2. Present the first scenario. Have students stand next to their desks and tell them they are going to jog in place for 1 minute.

3. Start the timer and have students jog for 1 minute.

4. Ask students if it seemed like a long time or not.

5. Tell them they will do it again, but you will let them know when they have completed part of the time. Make sure to clarify that 30 seconds is $\frac{1}{2}$ of a minute. Ask if they would like to know when they have jogged for $\frac{1}{4}$ of a minute, and clarify that this will happen after 15 seconds.

6. Start the timer again and let students know each time they have completed $\frac{1}{4}$ of a minute. Make sure you tell students after they have completed each $\frac{1}{4}$ of a minute without specifying how many $\frac{1}{4}$s are in 1 minute. You can do this by saying something like, "One-fourth of a minute has passed. Another fourth of a minute has passed," and so on, instead of saying, "One-fourth of a minute has passed. Two-fourths of a minute have passed," and so on.

This illustrates Strategy #2 of the ten essential strategies for supporting fraction sense: *Provide opportunities for students to investigate, assess, and refine mathematical "rules" and generalizations.* To learn more about this strategy, see Chapter 2 of *Beyond Pizzas & Pies: 10 Essential Strategies for Supporting Fraction Sense, Grades 3–5, Second Edition* (McNamara and Shaughnessy 2015).

This illustrates Strategy #10 of the ten essential strategies for supporting fraction sense: *Provide opportunities for students to build on their reasoning and sense-making skills about fractions by working with a variety of manipulatives and tools, such as Cuisenaire rods, Pattern Blocks, Fraction Kits, and ordinary items from their lives.* To learn more about this strategy, see Chapters 1, 3, and 4 of *Beyond Pizzas & Pies: 10 Essential Strategies for Supporting Fraction Sense, Grades 3–5, Second Edition* (McNamara and Shaughnessy 2015).

Introducing Activity 7.2: How Long? How Far?

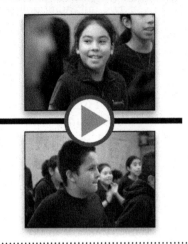

In this clip, we see Mr. Trenado's students beginning Activity 7.2. The activity starts with students jogging in place for 1 minute with no indication of how much time has elapsed. The students jog in place for a second minute, but this time are told each time they have completed $\frac{1}{4}$ of a minute. How do the two experiences prepare students for fraction division?

To view this video clip, scan the QR code or access via http://hein.pub/MathOLR

For commentary on the above, see the Appendix: Author's Video Reflections.

7. Instruct students to return to their seats and think about how the first experience (no interim time information) compared with the second experience (telling them when each $\frac{1}{4}$ minute passed).

Comparing the Two Jogging Experiences

In this clip, Mr. Trenado's students share their experiences with the two situations, jogging for 1 minute with no information about how much time had elapsed and jogging for 1 minute with information about how much time had elapsed. What different ways did students use the information in the second experience to reason about how much longer they needed to jog?

To view this video clip, scan the QR code or access via http://hein.pub/MathOLR

For commentary on the above, see the Appendix: Author's Video Reflections.

8. Ask students, "How many of the shorter periods ($\frac{1}{4}$ minute) did you complete in 1 minute?"

9. Then, ask students, "What division problem did you solve?" They may say $60 \div 15$. Acknowledge that this is one way of thinking about the problem. Ask if there is another way. If no one offers a suggestion, explain that because the unit they were working with was 1 minute, the problem was actually $1 \div \frac{1}{4}$.

10. Introduce the two-unit number lines and Cuisenaire rods. (See Figure 7–3; also available as Reproducibles A and B.) Tell students that one way to think about the answer to the problem $1 \div \frac{1}{4}$ is to ask themselves the question, "How many one-fourths are in one?"

11. Show a 24-centimeter interval on the board and label it as the unit interval—in this case, 1 minute. Lay down the 6-centimeter (light-green) giant rods to show each $\frac{1}{4}$ in the interval. (You may find it helpful to connect to the status bar that students may have seen on computers.)

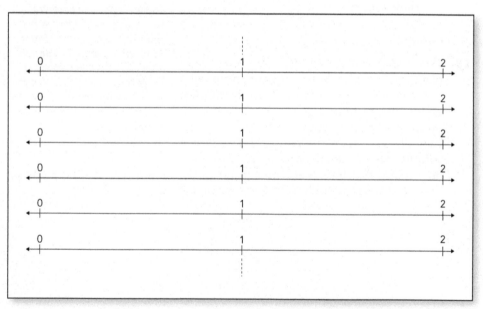

Figure 7–3. Two-Unit Number Lines (Reproducibles A and B, combined)

How Many $\frac{1}{4}$s Are in 1?

In this clip, we see both Carlos and Julian share their thinking with the class in answer to the question, "How many $\frac{1}{4}$s are in 1?" How does the combination of the context (finding out how many $\frac{1}{4}$ minutes are in 1 minute) and the materials (the Cuisenaire rods and the number line) help Carlos and Julian make sense of this problem?

To view this video clip, scan the QR code or access via http://hein.pub/MathOLR

For commentary on the above, see the Appendix: Author's Video Reflections.

12. Pass out the two-unit number lines and direct students to work with their partner and use their number lines and Cuisenaire rods to show how there are four $\frac{1}{4}$ minutes in 1 minute.

13. Tell students that they don't have to jog in place again, but you want them to imagine that they were going to do it for 2 minutes, and you want to find out how many $\frac{1}{4}$-minute intervals they would have to complete. Extend the line on the board and ask for a volunteer to use the Cuisenaire rods to show how many $\frac{1}{4}$ minutes are in 2 minutes. Have students do the same at their desks. Ask them how this shows that $2 \div \frac{1}{4} = 8$.

This illustrates Strategy #7 of the ten essential strategies for supporting fraction sense: *Provide opportunities for students to translate between different fraction representations.* To learn more about this strategy, see Chapter 7 of *Beyond Pizzas & Pies: 10 Essential Strategies for Supporting Fraction Sense, Grades 3–5, Second Edition* (McNamara and Shaughnessy 2015)

How Many $\frac{1}{4}$s Are in 2?

In this clip, we see Paloma and her partner using the Cuisenaire rods to find how many $\frac{1}{4}$s are in 2. Paloma then shares her thinking with the class. How does her discussion with her partner prepare Paloma to share her thinking with the class?

To view this video clip, scan the QR code or access via http://hein.pub/MathOLR

For commentary on the above, see the Appendix: Author's Video Reflections.

14. Write $2 \div \frac{1}{3}$ on the board and ask students to solve using either the Cuisenaire rods or another method. Have students share responses.

How Many $\frac{1}{3}$s Are in 2?

After Mr. Trenado introduces the problem, we see Yennifer and Ivelisse discussing the problem. How does Ivelisse use her understanding of how many $\frac{1}{3}$s are in 1 to determine how many $\frac{1}{3}$s are in 2?

To view this video clip, scan the QR code or access via http://hein.pub/MathOLR

For commentary on the above, see the Appendix: Author's Video Reflections.

15. Write $2 \div \frac{2}{3}$ on the board and ask students to solve using either the Cuisenaire rods or another method. Have students share responses.

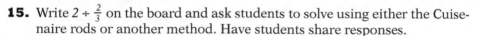

16. Wrap up by asking students some mental math problems such as $1 \div \frac{1}{6}$, $2 \div \frac{1}{6}$, $10 \div \frac{2}{3}$, and $10 \div \frac{3}{4}$. Have students share their responses.

17. Tell students that all the problems they have solved so far involve whole numbers divided by fractions, and write the equations on the board. Ask students what they notice about the quotients. Have students complete the sentence: When you divide a whole number by a fraction, the quotient is _____ [greater than, less than] both the dividend and the divisor.

This illustrates Strategy #2 of the ten essential strategies for supporting fraction sense: Provide opportunities for students to investigate, assess, and refine mathematical "rules" and generalizations. To learn more about this strategy, see Chapter 2 of Beyond Pizzas & Pies: 10 Essential Strategies for Supporting Fraction Sense, Grades 3–5, Second Edition (McNamara and Shaughnessy 2015).

18. If you are not planning to continue on to Part II, return to the discussion at the beginning of the lesson about division. Ask students whether they would like to change any of the statements they made based on their recent experience. If you have time for Part II, save this question until the end of Part II.

Part II

19. Tell students they are now going to solve problems involving fractions divided by whole numbers.

20. Let them know that to help them think about the first problem, you are going to present a series of division problems involving whole numbers first. Present the problem $\frac{1}{2} \div 2$ and ask students what they think the answer is. Have students share their thinking. Suggest they think about whole-number division to help them consider the answer to $\frac{1}{2} \div 2$. Present the scenario of a beach cleanup, using the problems $8 \div 2$ (8 miles of beach, with 2 kids doing the cleanup, means each kid has 4 miles of beach to clean up), $4 \div 2$, $2 \div 2$, and $1 \div 2$ in order and draw students' attention to the patterns of the quotients. A table such as the one shown here may be useful:

Distance	Number of people	Each person cleans
8 miles	2	4 miles
4 miles	2	2 miles
2 miles	2	1 mile
1 mile	2	$\frac{1}{2}$ mile
$\frac{1}{2}$ mile	2	? mile

21. Suggest that the Cuisenaire rods can also be useful for finding the answer to $\frac{1}{2} \div 2$. Return to the number line from the jogging problem and ask for a volunteer to use Cuisenaire rods to show $\frac{1}{2}$ divided into two equal parts. Have students talk to each other to determine what to call one of the parts ($\frac{1}{4}$).

22. Present the next problem, $\frac{1}{3} \div 2$, using the same scenario of a beach clean-up, and have students solve it using the Cuisenaire rods. Ask how they know what to call the quotient.

23. Present the following problems and give students time to solve them, using the Cuisenaire rods or another method.

a. $\frac{1}{4} \div 3$

b. $\frac{1}{6} \div 2$

c. $\frac{1}{2} \div 3$

d. $\frac{3}{4} \div 3$

e. $\frac{2}{3} \div 6$

24. Tell students that all the problems they have solved so far involve fractions divided by whole numbers, and complete the equations on the board. Ask students what they notice about the quotients. Return to the discussion at the beginning of the lesson about division. Ask students if they would like to change any of the statements they made based on their recent experience.

All's Fair at the Math Fair

Materials

All's Fair at the Math Fair (**Reproducible 7a**), 1 per student

Overview

During this activity, students use a tape diagram to represent division in the context of creating ribbons for a school Math Fair. The importance of identifying the unit is emphasized as students solve the problems.

This illustrates Strategy #10 of the ten essential strategies for supporting fraction sense: *Provide opportunities for students to build on their reasoning and sense-making skills about fractions by working with a variety of manipulatives and tools, such as Cuisenaire rods, Pattern Blocks, Fraction Kits, and ordinary items from their lives.* To learn more about this strategy, see Chapters 1, 3, and 4 of *Beyond Pizzas & Pies: 10 Essential Strategies for Supporting Fraction Sense, Grades 3–5, Second Edition* (McNamara and Shaughnessy 2015).

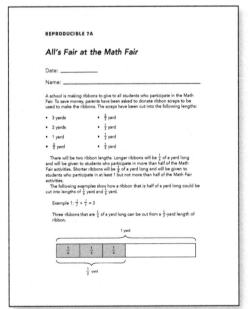

Figure 7–4. *All's Fair at the Math Fair*

1. Hand out *All's Fair at the Math Fair* and present the following scenario to students. (See Figure 7–4; also available as Reproducible 7a.) Allow time for students to think on their own first about how they might solve it, and then have them discuss their ideas with a partner:

A school is making ribbons to give to all students who participate in the Math Fair. To save money, parents have been asked to donate ribbon scraps to be used to make the ribbons. The scraps have been cut into the following lengths:

- 3 yards
- 2 yards
- 1 yard
- $\frac{3}{4}$ yard
- $\frac{2}{3}$ yard
- $\frac{1}{2}$ yard
- $\frac{1}{3}$ yard
- $\frac{1}{4}$ yard

There will be two ribbon lengths. Longer ribbons will be $\frac{1}{6}$ of a yard long and will be given to students who participate in more than half of the Math Fair activities. Shorter ribbons will be $\frac{1}{8}$ of a yard long and will be given to students who participate in at least 1 but not more than half of the Math Fair activities.

How many of each type of ribbon (full participation and partial participation) can be cut from each length of scrap ribbon? Use a tape diagram to show how each ribbon could be divided into the lengths described for the two levels of participation.

2. The examples shown here demonstrate how a ribbon that is $\frac{1}{2}$-yard long could be cut into lengths of $\frac{1}{6}$ of a yard and $\frac{1}{8}$ of a yard.

Example 1: $\frac{1}{2} \div \frac{1}{6} = 3$

Three ribbons that are $\frac{1}{6}$ of a yard long can be cut from a $\frac{1}{2}$-yard length of ribbon. (See Figure 7–5.)

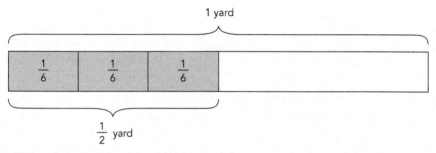

Figure 7–5. Tape diagram showing $\frac{1}{2} \div \frac{1}{6}$.

Example 2: $\frac{1}{2} \div \frac{1}{8} = 4$

Four ribbons that are $\frac{1}{8}$ of a yard long can be cut from a $\frac{1}{2}$-yard length of ribbon. (See Figure 7–6.)

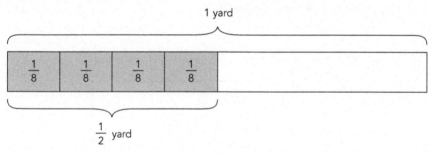

Figure 7–6. Tape diagram showing $\frac{1}{2} \div \frac{1}{8}$.

3. Have students work on the problems with a partner or small group and prepare to report back regarding how many of each type of ribbon (full participation or partial participation) can be made from each length of ribbon.

4. Students in need of an additional challenge can work on the extension problem.

All's Fair Extension

The school is making an effort to cut down on waste. How would you rec-ommend cutting the ribbons to have the greatest number of both types of ribbons (full participation and partial participation) with the least amount of ribbon going to waste?

7.4 Divide (or Multiply) and Conquer!

Overview

This game is a variation on the popular card game *War*. Student pairs choose whether they should divide or multiply a pair of numbers to create the greatest quotient or product. The team with the greatest quotient or product keeps the cards. The goal of the game is to collect the most cards.

Materials

Divide (or Multiply) and Conquer! cards (**Reproducible 7b**), 1 set per group of 4 students

1. Tell students they will be playing the game *Divide (or Multiply) and Conquer!* in teams of two against another team of two.

2. Teach the game by asking four students to demonstrate. Pair the students up and explain that each pair will be a team.

3. Deal out the cards facedown into three piles. One pile is for the Starter Card, one pile is for Team A, and one pile is for Team B. (See Figure 7–7; also available as Reproducible 7b.)

REPRODUCIBLE 7B

Divide (or Multiply) and Conquer! Cards

2	2	3
3	4	4
6	6	12
$\frac{1}{2}$	$\frac{1}{2}$	$\frac{1}{2}$
$\frac{1}{2}$	$\frac{1}{2}$	$\frac{1}{3}$

Figure 7–7. *Divide (or Multiply) and Conquer!* Cards

4. One student turns over the top card of the Starter Card pile. The number on this card will be either the multiplier or dividend with which each team will work. For example, if the card says $\frac{1}{3}$, then $\frac{1}{3}$ will be the first number in the equation that each team will solve.

This illustrates Strategy #9 of the ten essential strategies for supporting fraction sense: *Provide opportunities for students to engage in mathematical discourse and share and discuss their mathematical ideas, even those that may not be fully formed or completely accurate.* To learn more about this strategy, see Chapter 8 of *Beyond Pizzas & Pies: 10 Essential Strategies for Supporting Fraction Sense, Grades 3–5, Second Edition* (McNamara and Shaughnessy 2015).

5. Each team then picks the top card from its pile but does not show the card to the other team.

6. After looking at their card, the team members discuss which operation they want to use—multiplication or division—to get the highest result. For example, if the members of Team A pick a card that says $\frac{1}{6}$, they can either multiply $\frac{1}{3}$ (the Starter Card) by $\frac{1}{6}$ or divide $\frac{1}{3}$ by $\frac{1}{6}$. Because the goal is to get the highest number, they would choose divide, which results in a score of 2, because $\frac{1}{3} \div \frac{1}{6} = 2$.

7. At the same time, Team B draws a card from its pile, looks at the number, and discusses which operation to use. For example, if Team B's card says 2, the team members would select multiplication as their operation. They would end this round with a score of $\frac{2}{3}$, because $\frac{1}{3} \times 2 = \frac{2}{3}$.

8. After each round, the team with the highest score collects all three cards. In the case of a tie, shuffle all three cards (the Starter Card, Team A's card, and Team B's card) and place one card back into each of the three piles.

9. Play continues in this manner with a new Starter Card and each team choosing a new card from its pile.

10. When all the cards have been used, the team with the most cards is declared the winner.

Dividing fractions has, historically, been a challenging concept for students and teachers. Most instruction on the topic has focused on the divide-and-multiply algorithm only, with little attention given to (1) understanding what it means to divide fractions and (2) understanding the mathematics behind the algorithm. Helping students connect what they know about whole-number division to division with fractions is essential. Encouraging them to identify patterns, estimate quotients, defend their answers, and explore the relationship between multiplication and division is a necessary aspect of making this connection.

Study Questions

After Reading Chapter 7

1. What information presented in the "Classroom Scenario," "What's the Math?," and "What's the Research?" sections was familiar to you or similar to your experience with students?

2. Using one's knowledge of whole-number division to understand fraction division is a somewhat different approach to dividing fractions than we have seen in the past. How will this change influence how you approach fraction division with your students?

3. Which of the Classroom Activities (Activity 7.1: *Division Patterns*, Activity 7.2: *How Long? How Far?*, Activity 7.3: *All's Fair at the Math Fair*, Activity 7.4: *Divide [or Multiply] and Conquer!*) do you plan to implement with your students?

After Trying One or More of the Activities

1. Describe the activity and any modifications you made to meet your students' needs or align with your curriculum.

2. How did this activity add to your knowledge of what your students do and do not understand about division with fractions?

3. What are your next steps for supporting your students' learning about fraction division?

Connections to *Beyond Pizzas & Pies, Second Edition*

Beyond Invert & Multiply builds on the foundational understandings introduced in its companion resource, *Beyond Pizzas & Pies, Second Edition*. I recommend pairing this chapter with Chapters 1, 2, and 7 in *Beyond Pizzas & Pies, Second Edition* to continue your learning.

Discourse with Fractions

Developing Awareness

Six Strategies for Fostering Student Talk About Fractions

OUTLINE

Recently, I attended a session at a statewide math conference aimed at encouraging students to engage in meaningful discourse in math class. The presenter led us through an activity involving creating designs with pattern blocks. After we had all created our own designs, we were instructed to get up from our seats and do a "walk-around" to view and discuss how others had solved the problem. After returning to our seats, the presenter asked for comments and questions about the experience. Participants shared insights such as the following:

- "It was really great getting to solve the problem on my own first and then see how others did it."
- "Talking with others about how they solved the problem was a really good way to encourage us to use academic language."
- "My English learners would feel really comfortable talking during the walk-around because it would feel less formal than a whole-class discussion."
- "This is a great way to prepare students to participant in a whole-class discussion."

One of the participants raised her hand and asked, "But doesn't it get noisy? I mean, isn't there a lot of talking during the walk-around?" The presenter paused briefly before addressing this question. She then went on to say, "Yes, it does get noisy and yes, if I've prepared them well enough, students will do a lot of talking." She added that the structure of the lesson was designed specifically to encourage students to talk to one another about the mathematics of the task. She identified several strategies that she incorporated into the lesson to make this possible, including (1) allowing students time to work on the task on their own before discussing the task with others, (2) providing materials for students to use to complete the task, (3) providing time for students to view how others solved the task, and (4) creating a safe, low-pressure environment during which students were encouraged to talk about the task in pairs or small groups.

The strategies the presenter used in the lesson are just a few of the many that teachers have found successful in encouraging students to engage in discourse in math class. In this chapter, I address six additional strategies that have been found to support students to share their mathematical thinking on fractions with their peers. These strategies are illustrated by clips from the activities featured in the previous chapters. This is by no means an exhaustive list; however, I am hopeful that you'll find these strategies to be a great start in fostering student talk about fractions in your classroom.

I f you want students to talk, you've got to give them something to talk about! Tasks that are particularly good for fostering discourse are somewhat puzzling, open-ended, open to multiple solution paths and/or solutions, and encourage student reasoning. On the contrary, tasks that are less conducive to encouraging discourse focus on the correct implementation of a formalized procedure.

VIDEO CLIP 8a

Multiplication Patterns

In this clip, we see students building on their previous work with whole number multiplication to estimate the answer to multiplication problems involving fractions. Why is this a good task for beginning students' work with fraction multiplication?

To view this video clip, scan the QR code or access via http://hein.pub/MathOLR

For commentary on the above, see the Appendix: Author's Video Reflections.

Strategy 1: Using Strategic Tasks

As students work with more complex mathematical ideas, they may need to create a record of their thinking as a support for their verbal explanations. This is particularly true of students who are not used to sharing their thinking verbally or who struggle with language. The record of thinking acts as a road map for students and provides them with visual cues around which to focus their explanation. In addition to helping students explain reasoning and strategies, records of thinking can also provide insight for you and other students as students' thinking is made public. New technologies, such as document cameras, tablets, and smart boards, are useful tools for sharing students' ideas. In the absence of such technologies, however, personal whiteboards and student-created posters can be just as useful.

VIDEO CLIP 8b

Muhammad's Strategy for Adding $\frac{5}{9}$ and $\frac{8}{9}$

In this clip, Lupe asks for help adding $\frac{5}{9}$ and $\frac{8}{9}$. We see Muhammad explaining his strategy for solving the problem. How does the written record of his work support Muhammad's explanation and help Lupe understand his strategy?

To view this video clip, scan the QR code or access via http://hein.pub/MathOLR

For commentary on the above, see the Appendix: Author's Video Reflections.

n the same way that records of thinking can provide support for students to engage in mathematical discourse, providing students with visual models can also scaffold students' efforts to share their thinking. Concrete materials, such as Cuisenaire rods and fraction strips, and mathematical representations such as number lines, can be especially powerful tools, particularly if they address mathematical concepts in ways that are authentic as well as generalizable.

VIDEO CLIP 8c

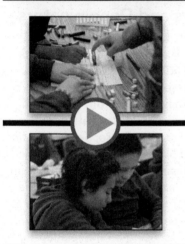

Using the Cuisenaire Rods to Explain Equivalent Fractions

In this clip, we see how Carlos uses the Cuisenaire rods to explain to his partner his reasoning about different ways to partition 1 minute (60 seconds). What ways does he share? How do the Cuisenaire rods support Carlos as he moves back and forth fluidly between the units of time—in other words, 1 minute and 60 seconds, and the fractional equivalents?

To view this video clip, scan the QR code or access via http://hein.pub/MathOLR

For commentary on the above, see the Appendix: Author's Video Reflections.

Understanding benchmark numbers is an important aspect of developing number sense. This is no less true when working with fractions than it is when working with whole numbers. Reasoning about benchmark fractions can provide opportunities for students to discover, test, and generalize relationships between their numerators and denominators. In addition, students can use benchmark fractions, such as $\frac{1}{2}$ and 1, to compare fractions and estimate the results of fraction computation.

VIDEO CLIP 8d

What Do You Notice About the Numerators and Denominators of Fractions Equal to $\frac{1}{2}$?

Providing explicit opportunities for students to develop an understanding of benchmark fractions is an essential aspect of fraction instruction. This clip comes from a lesson in *Beyond Pizza & Pies: 10 Essential Strategies for Supporting Fraction Sense, Second Edition* (McNamara and Shaughnessy 2015), in which students use Cuisenaire rods to partition number lines; chart fractions that are equal to, less than, and greater than $\frac{1}{2}$; and focus on the relationships between numerators and denominators. How can focusing on the relationship between numerators and denominators help students use $\frac{1}{2}$ as a benchmark fraction?

To view this video clip, scan the QR code or access via http://hein.pub/MathOLR

For commentary on the above, see the Appendix: Author's Video Reflections.

Sometimes, no matter how well you've set up a task, when you pose a question to students you do not get the lively conversation you were hoping you'd get. In *Classroom Discussions in Math: A Teacher's Guide for Using Talk Moves to Support the Common Core and More, Third Edition* (Chapin, O'Connor, and Anderson 2013), the authors identify research-based moves that teachers can make to support students' engagement in mathematical discourse. These talk moves have been embedded throughout the video clips shared in the book thus far; this section presents several more video clips that allow us to think specifically about some of the moves.

Revoicing

Revoicing: repeating what students have said

This strategy provides students with a second opportunity to hear and process their classmates' ideas. It is also a chance (1) for teachers to make sure they fully understand students' statements and (2) to help students refine or develop their ideas further.

VIDEO CLIP 8e

Ms. Lee Revoices Ashley's Justification

This clip takes place in the middle of a discussion of multiplication patterns. Students have solved the problems 6×8, 6×4, 6×2, and 6×1, and are discussing what 6 should be multiplied by next. After Ashley agrees that the next problem should be $6 \times \frac{1}{2}$, we hear the teacher revoicing her justification, based on the pattern of the previous problems. What purposes might Ms. Lee have had in revoicing Ashley's justification?

To view this video clip, scan the QR code or access via http://hein.pub/MathOLR

For commentary on the above, see the Appendix: Author's Video Reflections.

Repeating

Repeating: asking students to restate someone else's reasoning

Much like revoicing, this move provides another opportunity for students to hear the ideas of their classmates. It also encourages the participation of additional students, as students are often more comfortable repeating a classmate's ideas than sharing their own. In addition, this strategy sends a clear message to students that they have a responsibility to speak so that others can understand, and to listen and respond to the ideas of their classmates.

VIDEO CLIP 8f

Julian Restates Carlos's Answer

In this clip, which comes from Activity 7.2 in Chapter 7 (also labeled as Video Clip 7c), Carlos answers the question, "How many one-fourths are in one?" We then hear Mr. Trenado ask a student to restate Carlos's answer. What benefits might come from asking students to restate each others' ideas?

To view this video clip, scan the QR code or access via http://hein.pub/MathOLR

For commentary on the above, see the Appendix: Author's Video Reflections.

Reasoning

Reasoning: asking students to apply their own reasoning to someone else's reasoning

This move reinforces the idea that ideas in math class are to be shared, considered, and critiqued. It also supports the notion that partially formed ideas and incorrect responses can be valuable resources on the road to deep understanding.

VIDEO CLIP 8g

Multiple Students Share Their Reasoning About Placing $\frac{1}{2}$ on the Number Line

In this clip, which comes from Activity 1.3 in Chapter 1 (also labeled as Video Clip 1a), we watch as four students share their reasoning about where to place $\frac{1}{2}$ on a 0–4 number line. How do these ideas help shape the conversation and provide the teacher with important information about what students do and don't understand?

To view this video clip, scan the QR code or access via http://hein.pub/MathOLR

For commentary on the above, see the Appendix: Author's Video Reflections.

Adding On

Adding on: prompting students for further participation

As students begin to share their mathematical thinking with their peers, they likely do not have a good understanding of what makes a complete explanation. This is especially true with students whose previous experience with talking in math class consisted of providing one-word answers to closed questions posed by the teacher. To help students provide a more complete response, it may be necessary to prompt them to add more to their answers.

VIDEO CLIP 8h

"Tell Us More About That"

In this clip, Astrid tells the class that she knows that the answer to $6 \times 2\frac{1}{2}$ is between 12 and 20. The teacher prompts her to add on to her response by saying, "Tell us more about that." Astrid goes on to share how she came up with her answer. How does Ms. McNamara's prompt help the students understand what a complete answer involves?

To view this video clip, scan the QR code or access via http://hein.pub/MathOLR

For commentary on the above, see the Appendix: Author's Video Reflections.

Waiting

Waiting: using wait time

Of all of the teacher moves discussed thus far, using wait time is by far the easiest—at least in theory! Wait time is a perfect example of a practice that is what I call, "Simple, but not easy." Waiting to call on students for eight to ten seconds after posing a question is anything but easy. The research on wait time is very compelling. Just adding those few seconds before calling on students greatly increases the number and variety of responses you will get.

Chapin, O'Connor, and Anderson (2013) suggest using wait time in two ways. The first way is to wait for ten seconds after you've posed a question before you call on students. The second way is to allow students time to formulate their answers (the authors suggest thirty to forty seconds) after they've been called on. In addition, if students are still having trouble answering after giving them additional thinking time, tell them you'll come back to them in a few minutes. In this way, students know you expect them to keep trying and that their ideas are important.

VIDEO CLIP 8i

Posing a "Thinking Question"

In this clip, we see the introduction to a lesson in *Beyond Pizzas and Pies: 10 Essential Strategies for Supporting Fraction Sense, Second Edition* (McNamara and Shaughnessy 2015), in which students find the fractional relationships between different pattern blocks. To establish the idea that part–whole relationships depend on knowing both the part and the whole, students are asked to provide the fraction name for the triangle. The teacher provides several seconds for students to come up with an answer, telling them that this is a "thinking question." After several students have provided ideas, the teacher continues by establishing the idea that to know the fraction name for the triangle, you must also know which pattern block is being used as the whole. What is the purpose of wait time and how does it help students in this clip?

To view this video clip, scan the QR code or access via http://hein.pub/MathOLR

For commentary on the above, see the Appendix: Author's Video Reflections.

Sometimes, no matter how well you prepare the task, how much wait time you provide, and how many tools students have at their disposal, students may still be hesitant to volunteer an answer to your questions. Turn and talk is a strategy that is used throughout the video clips in this book and is especially beneficial with students who may need extra time formulating their response, extra practice expressing their ideas, and extra opportunities hearing how others are thinking about the task. Turn and talk can be used at any time throughout a lesson, depending on your goal. At the beginning of a task, turn and talk can help students generate multiple ideas and spark students' interest; after students have had time to work on a task, turn and talk allows them to hear how others approached the task and to compare their strategies. Using turn and talk before students are asked to share their current thinking provides opportunities for students to practice and refine their responses.

VIDEO CLIPS
6d, 6f, 7d, and 7e

Teachers' Use of Turn and Talk

Revisit these clips. Each clip shows teachers using turn and talk as a strategy for preparing students to share their thinking during whole-class discussion. You will see how several of the strategies included in this chapter are just as beneficial to students when they talk in small groups as they are when they are engaged in discussion with the whole class. What impact might the use of turn and talk have on students' contributions to whole-group discussions?

For commentary on the above, see the Appendix: Author's Video Reflections.

The third Standard for Mathematical Practice from the Common Core State Standards for Mathematics states that students "[c]onstruct viable arguments and critique the reasoning of others" (National Governors Association Center for Best Practices and the Council of State School Officers 2010). For students to do this, teachers must provide students with interesting tasks, use strategies that support students' reasoning, and provide time for students to engage in meaningful discourse. For many students, this will be a very different type of math class than they have experienced in the past. For these strategies to be successful, it is essential that students and teachers understand the value of engaging in mathematical discourse, and that they also understand that learning to engage in such discourse takes time, practice, and focused effort. For teachers, this means students need multiple opportunities to practice using the strategies; for students, this means they need multiple opportunities to share their reasoning. Last, as with all learning, it is essential that teachers and students understand that with practice comes progress, and that thinking, reasoning, and refining are at the heart of understanding.

Study Questions

After Reading Chapter 8

1. Sharing and justifying their mathematical thinking can be challenging for many students. What hurdles come to mind when thinking about using these strategies in your classroom?

2. Which of the strategies from this chapter (Using Strategic Tasks, Creating Records of Thinking, Building Visual Models, Reasoning with Benchmarks and the Number Line, Using Talk Moves, Asking Students to Turn and Talk) do you plan to implement with your students?

Acknowledgments

My interest in the teaching and learning of fractions began as a class-room teacher in Vallejo, California, and gained focus when I was a doctoral student in the Graduate School of Education at the University of California, Berkeley. I thank my graduate advisors, Geoffrey Saxe and Maryl Gearhart, for encouraging me to focus my graduate studies on this topic. My dissertation, and that of coauthor Meghan Shaughnessy, contributed to our resource *Beyond Pizzas & Pies: 10 Essential Strategies for Supporting Fraction Sense, Second Edition* (2015), the first edition of which was originally published in 2010. I thank Meghan for continuing to help me think through these ideas and her willingness to discuss the teaching and learning of fractions under a variety of circumstances and settings—on a running trail, over a glass of wine, via email, or in the context of our work with teacher candidates, to name a few. I also thank the other educators and researchers whose work appears in this resource. Your expertise informs my work on a daily basis.

I also thank the wonderful people at Math Solutions for their ongoing support and enthusiasm. Jamie Cross and Denise Botelho have been incredibly patient and open to my vision for the book. I so appreciated having Carolyn Felux, Patty Clark, Kelli Cook, and Patricio Dujan on site during the filming of the lessons for the video clips. And of course Doris Hirschhorn, who read through the manuscript with a fine-toothed comb and always pushed me to ensure that my ideas were clear, correct, and understandable to the reader.

I thank the crew at Friday's Films who treat the work of teaching and learning with tremendous respect and were a delight to work with.

Many teachers and students contributed to the research and activities in this book. I thank Carolyn Gramstorff and her teachers at North Oakland Community Charter School in Oakland, California, for allowing me to administer assessments to their students to add to my understanding of students' ideas about fractions. I also thank Karen Thompson and her wonderful fifth graders at Farrand Elementary in Plymouth, Michigan, for providing invaluable feedback on an early version of *Fractions Greater Than 1*.

I thank administrators, Steve Sexton and Yanira Canizales, at Lighthouse Community Charter School in Oakland, California, for allowing me to bring a film crew into their school. The lessons included in the video clips would not have been possible without their support as well as the support and enthusiasm of the wonderful teachers at Lighthouse. Laura Kretschmar, Emily Lee, and Huber Trenado generously allowed me, and a film crew, to disrupt precious instructional time to prepare for and film the lessons. I thank the parents and guardians for allowing their students to participate in the lessons. Most important, I thank the students for their hard work, persistence, and excitement about learning. Everyone who watches you will learn from your examples!

Finally I thank my family, without whom none of this would be possible. Every word, number, and graphic on every page has been discussed, read, critiqued, refined, and revised through your help. Thanks for your patience, support, and wisdom.

Reproducibles

The following reproducibles are referenced and used with individual activities. These reproducibles are also available for downloadable, printable format at at http://hein.pub/MathOLR. See page xxviii in the frontmatter to register your title using the key code BIM.

Add It Up, Version 1

Date: _____

Name: _____

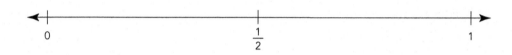

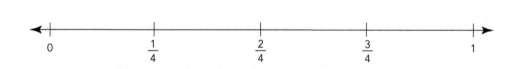

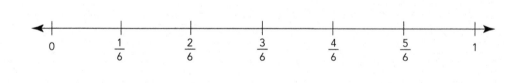

Add It Up, Version 2

Date: _____

Name: _____

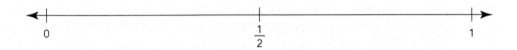

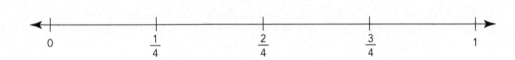

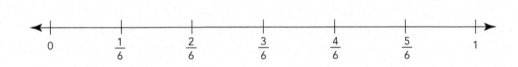

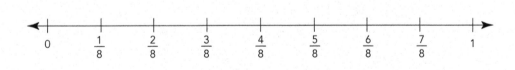

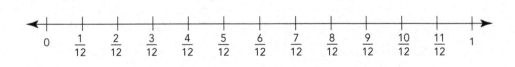

Fractions Greater Than 1

Date: _____

Name: _____

Directions

1. Cut out your number line and match the ends carefully so you have a continuous line from 0 to 4. Each unit interval must be the same length!
2. Glue your number line onto the sentence strip and write *1*, *2*, and *3* in the correct places below the line.
3. Cut out the mixed numbers and equivalent fractions carefully on the dotted lines.
4. Work with your partner to decide where on the number line each number should be placed.
5. When you both agree on the placement, glue the numbers on the line. *Whole and mixed numbers go below the line; equivalent fractions go above the line.*
6. After placing your mixed numbers and equivalent fractions in the right place, make sure you write the correct mixed number or equivalent fraction in the appropriate place above or below the line.

Example

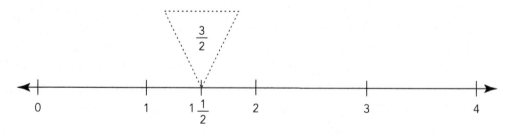

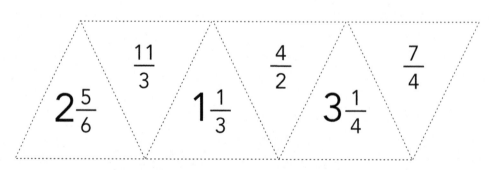

From *Beyond Invert & Multiply* by Julie McNamara. Portsmouth, NH: Heinemann. © 2015 by Heinemann. May be photocopied for classroom use.

0

4

Fraction Cards, Set A

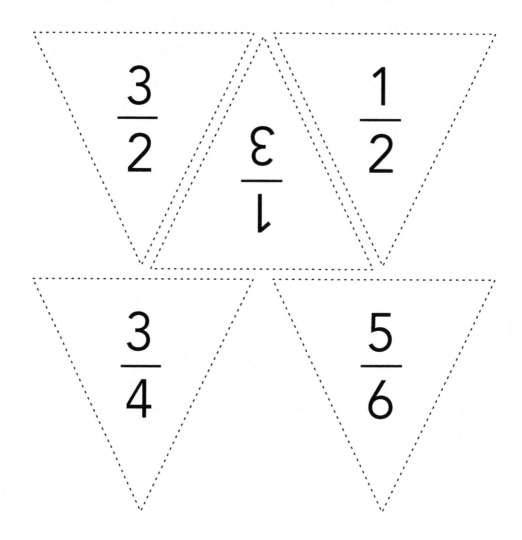

Fraction Cards, Set B

1	$\dfrac{1}{2}$	$\dfrac{1}{4}$
$\dfrac{3}{4}$	$\dfrac{1}{3}$	$\dfrac{2}{3}$
$\dfrac{1}{6}$	$\dfrac{5}{6}$	$\dfrac{1}{8}$
$\dfrac{5}{8}$	$\dfrac{1}{5}$	$\dfrac{3}{10}$

Addition with Cuisenaire Rods, Version 1, Recording Sheet

Date: _____

Name: _____

Directions: Use the Cuisenaire rods to solve the following problems.

1. $\frac{3}{4}$ brown rod + $\frac{1}{4}$ brown rod = _____ brown rod(s).

2. $\frac{5}{8}$ brown rod + $\frac{5}{8}$ brown rod = _____ brown rod(s).

3. $\frac{3}{4}$ brown rod + $\frac{3}{8}$ brown rod = _____ brown rod(s).

4. $1\frac{1}{4}$ brown rods + $\frac{1}{4}$ brown rod = _____ brown rod(s).

5. $\frac{1}{2}$ brown rod + $2\frac{5}{8}$ brown rods = _____ brown rod(s).

6. $2\frac{1}{4}$ brown rods + $3\frac{3}{4}$ brown rods = _____ brown rod(s).

7. $1\frac{1}{4}$ brown rods + $2\frac{5}{8}$ brown rods = _____ brown rod(s).

8. $3\frac{5}{8}$ brown rods + $2\frac{3}{4}$ brown rods = _____ brown rod(s).

Addition with Cuisenaire Rods, Version 2, Recording Sheet

Directions: Use the Cuisenaire rods to solve the following problems.

1. $\frac{2}{5}$ orange rod + $\frac{4}{5}$ orange rod = _____ orange rod(s).

2. $\frac{3}{4}$ purple rod + $\frac{1}{2}$ purple rod = _____ purple rod(s).

3. $\frac{2}{3}$ dark green rod + $\frac{5}{6}$ dark green rod = _____ dark green rod(s).

4. $1\frac{1}{2}$ red rods + $1\frac{1}{2}$ red rods = _____ red rod(s).

5. $2\frac{1}{2}$ orange rods + $2\frac{4}{5}$ orange rods = _____ orange rod(s).

6. $2\frac{2}{3}$ dark green rods + $1\frac{1}{2}$ dark green rods = _____ dark green rod(s).

7. $1\frac{3}{5}$ orange rods + $2\frac{1}{2}$ orange rods = _____ orange rod(s).

8. $1\frac{1}{2}$ dark green rods + $3\frac{1}{3}$ dark green rods = _____ dark green rod(s).

Make a One, Recording Sheet

Date: _____

Name: _____

$$\frac{\Box}{\Box} + \frac{\Box}{\Box} + \frac{\Box}{\Box} + \frac{\Box}{\Box} + \frac{\Box}{\Box} = 1 \quad \underline{\hspace{1cm}} \text{Round 1}$$

$$\frac{\Box}{\Box} + \frac{\Box}{\Box} + \frac{\Box}{\Box} + \frac{\Box}{\Box} + \frac{\Box}{\Box} = 1 \quad \underline{\hspace{1cm}} \text{Round 2}$$

$$\frac{\Box}{\Box} + \frac{\Box}{\Box} + \frac{\Box}{\Box} + \frac{\Box}{\Box} + \frac{\Box}{\Box} = 1 \quad \underline{\hspace{1cm}} \text{Round 3}$$

$$\frac{\Box}{\Box} + \frac{\Box}{\Box} + \frac{\Box}{\Box} + \frac{\Box}{\Box} + \frac{\Box}{\Box} = 1 \quad \underline{\hspace{1cm}} \text{Round 4}$$

$$\frac{\Box}{\Box} + \frac{\Box}{\Box} + \frac{\Box}{\Box} + \frac{\Box}{\Box} + \frac{\Box}{\Box} = 1 \quad \underline{\hspace{1cm}} \text{Round 5}$$

Total Score _____

Make a One, Version 1, Cards

1	1	1	1
1	1	1	1
1	1	2	2
2	2	2	2
2	2	2	2

4	4	4	4
4	4	4	4
4	4	8	8
8	8	8	8
8	8	8	8

Make a One, Version 2, Cards

1	1	1	1
1	1	1	1
1	1	3	3
3	3	3	3
3	3	3	3

6	6	6	6
6	6	6	6
6	6	12	12
12	12	12	12
12	12	12	12

Make a One, Rules

You need:

- One deck of forty cards, ten each of 1s, 2s, 4s, and 8s (for Version 1)
- One deck of forty cards, ten each of 1s, 3s, 6s, and 12s (for Version 2)
- One *Make a One* Recording Sheet
- A partner and another pair to play with

Rules for Version 1

1. One person mixes the Version 1 deck of cards and leaves them facedown.
2. Each pair takes ten cards.
3. Use as many of your cards as you can to make fractions that add to 1. Write the fractions on your recording sheet and fill in your score. You score 1 point for each box you fill in when making your fractions.
4. When everyone has completed the round, return to Step 1 and continue.
5. Play five rounds and figure your total score. The team with the highest score wins.

Rules for Version 2

Play the same way as you do for Version 1, but use the Version 2 deck of cards.

Rules for Version 3

Play the same way as you do for Versions 1 and 2, but shuffle both decks of cards together and use all the cards.

Get to the Whole, Version 1, Recording Sheet

Date: _____

Name: _____

Directions: Use the space below each problem to use the "Get to the Whole" strategy to solve the following problems.

1. $\frac{3}{10} + \frac{9}{10}$

2. $2\frac{5}{8} + \frac{5}{8}$

3. $\frac{5}{12} + 5\frac{11}{12}$

4. $\frac{3}{6} + \frac{5}{6}$

5. $\frac{7}{9} + 2\frac{5}{9}$

6. $\frac{2}{5} + \frac{4}{5}$

7. $1\frac{3}{4} + 2\frac{3}{4}$

8. $3\frac{5}{8} + 2\frac{7}{8}$

Get to the Whole, Version 2, Recording Sheet

Date: _____

Name: _____

Directions: Use the space below each problem to use the "Get to the Whole" strategy to solve the following problems.

1. $\frac{3}{10} + \frac{4}{5}$

2. $2\frac{5}{6} + \frac{5}{12}$

3. $\frac{1}{6} + 5\frac{11}{12}$

4. $\frac{1}{2} + \frac{5}{8}$

5. $\frac{3}{4} + \frac{2}{3}$

6. $\frac{1}{2} + \frac{4}{5}$

7. $1\frac{3}{4} + \frac{3}{6}$

8. $\frac{7}{12} + 2\frac{7}{8}$

Subtraction with Cuisenaire Rods, Version 1, Recording Sheet

Date: _____

Name: _____

Directions: Use the Cuisenaire rods to solve the following problems.

1. $\frac{3}{4}$ brown rod − $\frac{2}{4}$ brown rod = _____ brown rod(s).

2. $\frac{5}{8}$ brown rod − $\frac{1}{8}$ brown rod = _____ brown rod(s).

3. $\frac{3}{4}$ brown rod − $\frac{3}{8}$ brown rod = _____ brown rod(s).

4. $3\frac{1}{4}$ brown rods − $\frac{1}{2}$ brown rod = _____ brown rod(s).

5. $2\frac{5}{8}$ brown rods − $\frac{1}{2}$ brown rod = _____ brown rod(s).

6. $3\frac{1}{4}$ brown rods − $1\frac{3}{8}$ brown rods = _____ brown rod(s).

7. $5\frac{1}{2}$ brown rods − $3\frac{7}{8}$ brown rods = _____ brown rod(s).

8. $3\frac{5}{8}$ brown rods − $2\frac{3}{4}$ brown rods = _____ brown rod(s).

Subtraction with Cuisenaire Rods, Version 2, Recording Sheet

Date: _____

Name: _____

Directions: Use the Cuisenaire rods to solve the following problems.

1. $\frac{4}{5}$ orange rod – $\frac{2}{5}$ orange rod = _____ orange rod(s).

2. $\frac{3}{4}$ purple rod – $\frac{1}{2}$ purple rod = _____ purple rod(s).

3. $1\frac{2}{3}$ dark green rods – $\frac{5}{6}$ dark green rod = _____ dark green rod(s).

4. 5 red rods – $1\frac{1}{2}$ red rods = _____ red rod(s).

5. $4\frac{1}{2}$ orange rods – $2\frac{4}{5}$ orange rods = _____ orange rod(s).

6. $2\frac{1}{3}$ dark green rods – $1\frac{1}{2}$ dark green rods = _____ dark green rod(s).

7. $2\frac{1}{2}$ orange rods – $1\frac{3}{5}$ orange rods = _____ orange rod(s).

8. $5\frac{1}{2}$ dark green rods – $3\frac{2}{3}$ dark green rods = _____ dark green rod(s).

What's the Difference?, Recording Sheet

Date: _____

Name: _____

Directions: Use the number line to solve each problem.

1. Kira's favorite cookie recipe needs $1\frac{1}{3}$ cups of sugar. Jeremy's favorite cookie recipe needs $\frac{2}{3}$ of a cup of sugar. How much more sugar does Kira's recipe need than Jeremy's?

2. Mariah and Grace are comparing how much they ran over the weekend to get in shape for soccer season. Mariah ran $4\frac{5}{8}$ of a mile. Grace ran $3\frac{3}{4}$ of a mile. How much farther did Mariah run than Grace?

3. Frankie walks $\frac{3}{5}$ of a mile to school. Albert walks $\frac{2}{3}$ of a mile to school. How much farther does Albert walk than Frankie?

4. Mr. Gregory is making his costume for the class play. The jacket needs $2\frac{1}{3}$ yards of fabric and the pants need $1\frac{3}{4}$ yards of fabric. How much more fabric does the jacket need than the pants?

5. Erik is working on his long jump. The school record is $10\frac{1}{2}$ feet. Erik can jump $8\frac{7}{8}$ feet. How many feet is Erik from matching the record?

The Race Is On!

Date: _____

Name: _____

Waterside School is holding a 15-mile relay race to raise money for a new library. Teams can consist of up to 30 people, as long as each participant on a team runs or walks the same distance. Mila and Max decide to make a team.

1. If Max and Mila don't find any friends to join them, how far will they each need to travel?

2. If Max's younger sister Marva decides to join the team, how far will they each need to travel?

3. Mila's cousin also decides to join the team. How far will each teammate need to travel now?

4. Max and Mila's team is getting very popular so they decide to create a chart to show how far each person on a team must travel for teams of any size, from 1 person to 30 people. Work with your group to complete a similar chart.

From *Beyond Invert & Multiply* by Julie McNamara. Portsmouth, NH: Heinemann. © 2015 by Heinemann. May be photocopied for classroom use.

All's Fair at the Math Fair

Date: _____

Name: _____

A school is making ribbons to give to all students who participate in the Math Fair. To save money, parents have been asked to donate ribbon scraps to be used to make the ribbons. The scraps have been cut into the following lengths:

- 3 yards
- 2 yards
- 1 yard
- $\frac{3}{4}$ yard

- $\frac{2}{3}$ yard
- $\frac{1}{2}$ yard
- $\frac{1}{3}$ yard
- $\frac{1}{4}$ yard

There will be two ribbon lengths. Longer ribbons will be $\frac{1}{6}$ of a yard long and will be given to students who participate in more than half of the Math Fair activities. Shorter ribbons will be $\frac{1}{8}$ of a yard long and will be given to students who participate in at least 1 but not more than half of the Math Fair activities.

The following examples show how a ribbon that is half of a yard long could be cut into lengths of $\frac{1}{6}$ yard and $\frac{1}{8}$ yard.

Example 1: $\frac{1}{2} \div \frac{1}{6} = 3$

Three ribbons that are $\frac{1}{6}$ of a yard long can be cut from a $\frac{1}{2}$-yard length of ribbon.

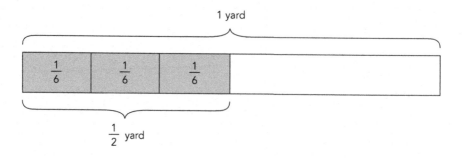

Example 2: $\frac{1}{2} \div \frac{1}{8} = 4$

Four ribbons that are $\frac{1}{8}$ of a yard long can be cut from a $\frac{1}{2}$-yard length of ribbon.

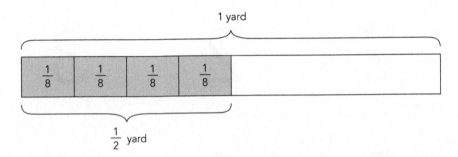

How many of each type of ribbon (full participation and partial participation) can be cut from each length of scrap ribbon? Use a tape diagram to show how each ribbon could be divided into the lengths described for the two levels of participation.

All's Fair Extension

The school is making an effort to cut down on waste. How would you recommend cutting the ribbons to have the greatest number of both types of ribbons (full participation and partial participation) with the least amount of ribbon going to waste?

Divide (or Multiply) and Conquer! Cards

2	2	3
3	4	4
6	6	12
$\frac{1}{2}$	$\frac{1}{2}$	$\frac{1}{2}$
$\frac{1}{2}$	$\frac{1}{2}$	$\frac{1}{3}$

$\dfrac{1}{3}$	$\dfrac{1}{3}$	$\dfrac{1}{3}$
$\dfrac{1}{3}$	$\dfrac{1}{4}$	$\dfrac{1}{4}$
$\dfrac{1}{4}$	$\dfrac{1}{4}$	$\dfrac{1}{4}$
$\dfrac{1}{6}$	$\dfrac{1}{6}$	$\dfrac{1}{6}$
$\dfrac{1}{6}$	$\dfrac{1}{12}$	$\dfrac{1}{12}$

Left Half of Two-Unit Number Lines

Date: _____

Name: _____

0   1

0   1

0   1

0   1

0   1

0   1

Right Half of Two-Unit Number Lines

Date: _____

Name: _____

1   2

1   2

1   2

1   2

1   2

1   2

From *Beyond Invert & Multiply* by Julie McNamara. Portsmouth, NH: Heinemann. © 2015 by Heinemann. May be photocopied for classroom use.

Author's Video Reflections

Video Clip Number/ Title/Grade/Teacher	Page Number	Introduction	Observations
1a Placing $\frac{1}{2}$ on the Number Line Grade 5/Ms. Kretschmar	16	This clip comes at the beginning of Activity 1.3. After Ms. Kretschmar shows students a four-unit number line with only the whole numbers 0 and 4 labeled, we see several students share their thinking about where to place $\frac{1}{2}$ on the line. Three different locations are suggested and discussed. What does Ms. Kretschmar learn about what students do and don't understand about fractions on the number line from the discussion?	Beginning the lesson with a number line with only the numbers 0 and 4 labeled allows Ms. Kretschmar to assess students' understanding of several aspects of the number line. When the first student places $\frac{1}{2}$ on the line (at the point where the number 2 should go), Ms. Kretschmar learns that she does understand what it means to partition a given length in half but is not considering $\frac{1}{2}$ as a number that falls between 0 and 1. The second student's placement of $\frac{1}{2}$ between 1 and 2 also provides insight into his understanding, as he is likely focusing on the individual digits of the numerator and denominator of the fraction and not on the coordination of digits that represents the number $\frac{1}{2}$. When the numbers 1, 2, and 3 are added to the number line we hear several students say, "Ah," highlighting an important number line principle that many seemed to miss at the beginning of the lesson—that is, the importance of identifying the unit interval (the distance from 0 to 1) when working with a multiunit number line.
1b Using Cuisenaire Rods to Place $\frac{1}{3}$ on the Number Line Grade 5/Ms. Kretschmar	17	In this clip, we see two students, Coleo and Juan, show where $\frac{1}{3}$ goes on the number line. Why does Ms. Kretschmar call on Juan to use the Cuisenaire rods to justify Coleo's placement? How does Juan's use of the Cuisenaire rods support students' understanding of placing fractions on the number line?	Coleo's placement of $\frac{1}{3}$ on the number line appears to be based on a visual estimate of where $\frac{1}{3}$ should go. Calling on Juan to come to the board and use the Cuisenaire rods to justify Coleo's placement serves three purposes. First, it reinforces the definition of $\frac{1}{3}$ as "the quantity formed by 1 part when a whole is partitioned into b (in this case, 3) equal parts" (NGO Center/CCSSO 2010). Second, it allows the other students to understand how the Cuisenaire rods can be used as useful tools for partitioning the number line. Third, it supports the mathematical practice of attending to precision, as Juan uses the rods to find a more precise placement for $\frac{1}{3}$ than afforded by Coleo's visual estimate.

Video Clip Number/Title/Grade/Teacher	Page Number	Introduction	Observations
1c Using Cuisenaire Rods to Place $\frac{3}{2}$ on the Number Line Grade 5/Ms. Kretschmar	18	In this clip, we see Samantha place $\frac{3}{2}$ on the number line. How does Samantha use the Cuisenaire rods to help her place the fraction?	Samantha first places two of the dark green rods below the number line, which takes her to 1. Since she doesn't have a third dark green rod she then moves one of the rods (thus showing three iterations of the length $\frac{1}{2}$) to determine where to place the number $\frac{3}{2}$.
1d Deciding Where to Place $\frac{11}{3}$ on the Number Line Grade 5/Ms. Kretschmar	19	In this clip, we hear from Braulio as he shares how he and his partner determined where to place $\frac{11}{3}$. How does Braulio draw on his understanding of unit fractions and whole numbers to decide which two whole numbers $\frac{11}{3}$ is between?	Braulio's explanation is based on his understanding that $\frac{3}{3}$ is equivalent to 1. He is able to explain how he mentally iterates $\frac{3}{3}$ two more times, which takes him to $\frac{9}{3}$ (or the whole number, 3). He knows he needs two more $\frac{1}{3}$s for a total of $\frac{11}{3}$; thus $\frac{11}{3}$ is between the whole numbers, 3 and 4.
3a Reviewing the "Make a 10" Strategy Grade 5/Ms. Kretschmar	51	In this clip, we see Ms. Kretschmar introducing Activity 3.4 by reminding students of the "Make a 10" strategy they used when playing "Oh No, 99!" How does reminding students of a successful strategy for whole number addition prepare them for success with fraction addition?	Too often, students (and teachers) approach instruction involving fractions as something completely new and different from their work with whole numbers. As a result, fraction computation is often performed with little reasoning or sense making. The Common Core calls for students to build on previous understandings of whole number operations as they solve problems involving fraction computation. As students work with fractions it is important that they understand that the strategies and properties of operations that they use flexibly and successfully with whole numbers can also be used when operating on fractions.
3b Introducing "Get to the Whole" Grade 5/Ms. Kretschmar	52	After reviewing the "Make a 10" strategy for working with whole numbers, Ms. Kretschmar introduces "Get to the Whole!" Why does Ms. Kretschmar select the fractions $\frac{3}{4}$ and $\frac{2}{5}$?	The selection of the fractions $\frac{3}{4}$ and $\frac{2}{5}$ prepares students to use the "Get to the Whole!" when adding fractions. When students are asked what they need to add to $\frac{3}{4}$ to "get to a whole" they draw on two concepts that are foundational to fraction computation. The first of these is that $\frac{4}{4}$ is equivalent to 1 (the closest whole number) and that $\frac{4}{4}$ is also composed of four $\frac{1}{4}$s. The same is true for $\frac{2}{5}$: The students use their understanding of the equivalence of $\frac{5}{5}$ and 1, as well as the fact that $\frac{5}{5}$ is composed of five $\frac{1}{5}$s.

(continued)

Video Clip Number/ Title/Grade/Teacher	Page Number	Introduction	Observations
3c $\frac{3}{4} + \frac{3}{4}$: Will's Strategy Grade 5/Ms. Kretschmar	53	In this clip, we see Will sharing his strategy for decomposing and recomposing $\frac{3}{4} + \frac{3}{4}$. What is Will's strategy? What mathematical properties does Will use in his strategy? What does Ms. Kretschmar do to help other students understand Will's thinking?	When students are sharing strategies verbally, there is always the risk that other students may not follow their thinking. In a classroom with many English language learners or students who are new to math discourse, this risk is even more pronounced. By questioning Will and recording his strategy, Ms. Kretschmar makes his thinking public. In this way, all students are able to access and make sense of where the $\frac{2}{4} + \frac{2}{4}$ came from in Will's strategy for decomposing and recomposing $\frac{3}{4} + \frac{3}{4}$. As Abigail restates Will's strategy, we see the impact of Ms. Kretschmar's follow-up with Will.
3d $\frac{3}{4} + \frac{3}{4}$: Belen's Strategy Grade 5/Ms. Kretschmar	53	In this clip, Ms. Kretschmar presses Belen to describe another strategy for decomposing and recomposing $\frac{3}{4} + \frac{3}{4}$. What is Belen's strategy, and how might students' previous use of the Cuisenaire rods have encouraged Belen's strategy?	To solve the problem $\frac{3}{4} + \frac{3}{4}$ Belen describes how the second $\frac{3}{4}$ could be broken up (or decomposed) into $\frac{2}{4}$ and $\frac{1}{4}$. As Belen speaks, we see the Cuisenaire rods on the board at the front of the room. Students' experience with using materials such as Cuisenaire rods can provide them with a visual model for understanding that $\frac{3}{4}$ is composed of three $\frac{1}{4}$s, and can be decomposed in more than one way to make addition (or subtraction) easier.
3e $\frac{3}{5} + \frac{4}{5}$: Malaya's Strategy Grade 5/Ms. Kretschmar	54	After students have discussed their strategies with a partner, we hear Malaya describe her strategy for adding $\frac{3}{5} + \frac{4}{5}$. What is Malaya's strategy and how does Ms. Kretschmar help other students understand Malaya's thinking?	As Malaya describes her strategy for adding $\frac{3}{5} + \frac{4}{5}$, Ms. Kretschmar presses her to make her decision making clear to the rest of the class. Malaya describes breaking apart the "four" because "three plus two equals five." Knowing that some students may be confused by Malaya's use of whole numbers (4, 3, 2, and 5) and may not understand where the numbers are coming from, Ms. Kretschmar reminds the students that the 4 is really "four-fifths." Ms. Kretschmar makes a mistake as she initially records Malaya's strategy, but knowing that it is important for the rest of the students to understand how Malaya decomposed and recomposed the numbers, she backs up and explicitly records how the numbers were decomposed and then added together to arrive at the sum.

Video Clip Number/ Title/Grade/Teacher	Page Number	Introduction	Observations
3f $\frac{3}{5} + \frac{4}{5}$: Yuli's Use of Academic Language Grade 5/Ms. Kretschmar	54	After hearing from Malaya, Ms. Kretschmar asks Yuli to share her strategy for adding $\frac{3}{5}$ and $\frac{4}{5}$. How does explaining her strategy to her classmates encourage Yuli's use of academic language?	Communicating one's thinking is a challenging but necessary component of today's classrooms. By explaining her strategy for adding $\frac{3}{5}$ and $\frac{4}{5}$ to her classmates, Yuli is presented with the need to communicate her thinking clearly. We hear her self-correct, as she first states that the answer is "One and one-whole," then "One and two-wholes," and then finally, the correct answer, "One and two-fifths."
6a Introducing Activity 6.1: Multiplication Patterns Grade 4/Ms. Lee	96	In this clip, we see Ms. Lee introducing Activity 6.1 to her fourth graders. Before addressing multiplication with fractions the activity begins with students solving multiplication problems involving whole numbers. How might starting with whole number multiplication help students solve fraction multiplication problems?	Too often, students (and teachers) approach instruction involving fractions as something completely new and different from their work with whole numbers. As a result, fraction computation is often performed with little reasoning or sense making. The Common Core calls for students to build on previous understandings of whole number operations as they solve problems involving fraction computation. As students work with fractions it is important that they understand that the strategies and properties of operations that they use flexibly and successfully with whole numbers can also be used when operating on fractions. Many students are likely to use repeated addition as one method for finding the products in the problems Ms. Lee shares. Starting with whole number multiplication prepares students to consider using similar strategies when multiplying fractions.
6b Noticing Patterns in Factors and Products Grade 4/Ms. Lee	97	In this clip, we hear Denise sharing what she noticed about the factors and products in the problems $6 \times 8 = 48$ and $6 \times 4 = 24$. How do Denise's observations prepare the other students to consider patterns they will encounter in subsequent problems ($6 \times 2, 6 \times 1, 6 \times \_\_\_$)?	Based on their previous experience with whole number multiplication, it is not surprising that students often believe that "multiplication always makes things bigger." Focusing on what happens to the products as the factors in the problems decrease in value (the products decrease in value by the same scale) prepares students to consider why $6 \times \frac{1}{2}$ results in a product that is less than 6.

(continued)

Video Clip Number/ Title/Grade/Teacher	Page Number	Introduction	Observations
6c Moving from Additive to Multiplicative Language Grade 4/Ms. Lee	97	In this clip, we see Emme sharing the pattern she noticed in the factors and products of the first three problems. How does Ms. Lee's rephrasing of Emme's observation help Emme's understanding?	As Ms. Lee rephrases Emme's contribution, she explicitly connects the multiplicative idea of doubling to the additive language Emme uses to first describe the pattern she notices ("Two plus two equals four" and "four plus four equals eight"). We hear Emme take this new language as her own when, in response to Ms. Lee's question about what she noticed about the products, Emme states, "They're also doubling."
6d What Number Is $\frac{1}{2}$ of 1? Grade 4/Ms. Lee	98	This clip comes after Ms. Lee has written $6 \times$ ____ on the board and asked students what number they think will go in the blank to continue the pattern. Many students respond to Ms. Lee's question by saying "zero." What does this response indicate about their understanding of $\frac{1}{2}$ as the number that would follow the pattern?	Even though Ms. Lee's students had been working with placing fractions on the number line (as shown on the board during the clip), their understanding of $\frac{1}{2}$ as the number that is half of 1 is negligible. By allowing students to talk with one another after asking them what number should go in the blank, Ms. Lee finds out that even students who understood the pattern when presented with whole numbers were thrown by the transition to fractions.
6e Multiplication as Repeated Addition Grade 4/Ms. Lee	99	After students have established that the next problem should be $6 \times \frac{1}{2}$, Ms. Lee models how repeated addition can be used to find the product of $6 \times \frac{1}{2}$. How might Ms. Lee's modeling here help students?	In early grades, students learn that many multiplication situations can be considered as "groups of" and solved by using repeated addition. Knowing that her students are familiar and comfortable with this strategy, Ms. Lee shows how $6 \times \frac{1}{2}$ can also be solved with repeated addition by adding $\frac{1}{2} + \frac{1}{2} + \frac{1}{2} + \frac{1}{2} + \frac{1}{2} + \frac{1}{2}$. She also helps students see how the associative property can be used to add the six $\frac{1}{2}$s together, by first adding $\frac{1}{2} + \frac{1}{2}$ three times, and then adding $1 + 1 + 1$ to arrive at the answer, 3.

Video Clip Number/ Title/Grade/Teacher	Page Number	Introduction	Observations
6f What Do We Know About $6 \times 2\frac{1}{2}$? Grade 4/Ms. McNamara	104	In this clip, we see fourth graders discussing what they know about the answer to $6 \times 2\frac{1}{2}$. How can this type of problem help students develop their understanding of mixed numbers?	By starting with the question, "What do you know about six multiplied by two and a half?" students are pushed to consider $2\frac{1}{2}$ as a number that is larger than 2 but less than 3. As students discuss their thinking about the problem, we hear evidence that some of them may not be quite there yet, and may in fact be interpreting $2\frac{1}{2}$ to mean two $\frac{1}{2}$s. By asking students to think about the problem before doing any calculations, teachers can gain valuable insights into students' understanding and target follow-up questions accordingly.
6g "$6 \times 2\frac{1}{2}$ Has to Be Greater Than $2\frac{1}{2}$" Grade 4/Ms. McNamara	104	In this clip, we see Lizette stating that the answer to $6 \times 2\frac{1}{2}$ has to be greater than $2\frac{1}{2}$. What important mathematical property is Lizette drawing on with this statement?	As Lizette tells the class that the answer to $6 \times 2\frac{1}{2}$ has to be more than $2\frac{1}{2}$, she is using her understanding of the identity property of multiplication, which states that any number times 1 is that number (or, $a \times 1 = a$). Understanding this property is essential as students create equivalent fractions by multiplying or dividing fractions by $\frac{n}{n}$ and use the standard (invert and multiply) algorithm for fraction division.
6h Applying the Distributive Property to Reason About the Product of $6 \times 2\frac{1}{2}$ Grade 4/Ms. McNamara	105	In this clip, we see two students sharing what they know about the answer to $6 \times 2\frac{1}{2}$. What do the students' responses indicate that they understand about multiplication and the distributive property?	The students intuitively use the distributive property as they provide justification for why $6 \times 2\frac{1}{2}$ will be greater than 12. Both students understand that in order to solve the problem, the $2\frac{1}{2}$ can be decomposed into $2 + \frac{1}{2}$, so that $6 \times 2\frac{1}{2}$ can be considered as $(6 \times 2) + (6 \times \frac{1}{2})$.
6i $4\frac{1}{2}$ Is More Than 4 But Less Than 5 Grade 4/Ms. McNamara	105	In this clip, Gregorio shares how he knows that $4\frac{1}{2} \times 5$ will be more than 20 and another student agrees with his reasoning. Why does Ms. McNamara ask Dat to share his rationale for thinking that $4\frac{1}{2} \times 5$ is less than 25?	Several students in this clip indicate their understanding that $4\frac{1}{2} \times 5$ will be more than 20 because $4\frac{1}{2}$ is more than 4 and $4 \times 5 = 20$. Ms. McNamara asks Dat to share his rationale for thinking that $4\frac{1}{2} \times 5$ is less than 25 to reinforce students' understanding the value of $4\frac{1}{2}$ and ensure that students understand that $4\frac{1}{2}$ is between the whole numbers 4 and 5.

(continued)

Video Clip Number/ Title/Grade/Teacher	Page Number	Introduction	Observations
7a Introducing Activity 7.2: How Long? How Far? Grade 6/Mr. Trenado and Ms. McNamara	128	In this clip, we see Mr. Trenado's students beginning Activity 7.2. The activity starts with students jogging in place for 1 minute with no indication of how much time has elapsed. The students jog in place for a second minute, but this time are told each time they have completed $\frac{1}{4}$ of a minute. How do the two experiences prepare students for fraction division?	Starting the lesson on fraction division with a situation that is familiar to students, such as jogging in place, provides them with a context that they can easily draw on as they consider the quotative interpretation of $1 \div \frac{1}{4}$ or, how many $\frac{1}{4}$ s are in 1? Jogging in place for even 1 minute can seem quite long, thus encouraging students to be thinking to themselves, "How much longer do we need to do this?" During the second minute of jogging students are primed to use the information about how many $\frac{1}{4}$ minutes have passed to help them reason about how many $\frac{1}{4}$ s are in 1 and how much longer they will be jogging.
7b Comparing the Two Jogging Experiences Grade 6/Mr. Trenado	129	In this clip, Mr. Trenado's students share their experiences with the two situations, jogging for 1 minute with no information about how much time had elapsed and jogging for 1 minute with information about how much time had elapsed. What different ways did students use the information in the second experience to reason about how much longer they needed to jog?	By having the students compare the two experiences (jogging for 1 minute without an indication of how much time has passed and jogging in place for 1 minute while being told each time $\frac{1}{4}$ of a minute has passed) the students are given motivation to consider the question of how many $\frac{1}{4}$ s are in 1. As students are wondering how much more time they will need to spend jogging, they are pressed to use what they know about the duration of $\frac{1}{4}$ of a minute, and then apply that understanding to determine how many $\frac{1}{4}$ s of a minute they will need to complete within the minute. Students use this information to tell them how much time has elapsed, and how much more time they still have to go.
7c How Many $\frac{1}{4}$ s Are in 1? Grade 6/Mr. Trenado	130	In this clip, we see both Carlos and Julian share their thinking with the class in answer to the question, "How Many $\frac{1}{4}$ s are in 1?" How does the combination of the context (finding out how many $\frac{1}{4}$ minutes are in 1 minute) and the materials (the Cuisenaire rods and the number line) help Carlos and Julian make sense of this problem?	We see both Carlos and Julian use the Cuisenaire rods in combination with the number line to represent the full minute (as shown by the tan rod) as well as $\frac{1}{4}$ minutes (the dark green rods) and $\frac{1}{4}$ minutes (the light green rods). The rods and the number line provide a concrete, visual model for the boys to manipulate as they consider the very abstract context of the duration of time. Having both Carlos and Julian share their thinking with the class gives students the opportunity to hear more than one explanation.

Video Clip Number/ Title/Grade/Teacher	Page Number	Introduction	Observations
7d How Many $\frac{1}{4}$s Are in 2? Grade 6/Ms. McNamara and Mr. Trenado	131	In this clip, we see Paloma and her partner using the Cuisenaire rods to find how many $\frac{1}{4}$s are in 2. Paloma then shares her thinking with the class. How does her discussion with her partner prepare Paloma to share her thinking with the class?	Paloma and her partner use the Cuisenaire rods to prove to each other and practice explaining that there are four $\frac{1}{4}$s in 1 and eight $\frac{1}{4}$s in 2. By working first with her partner, Paloma is well prepared to share her thinking with the rest of the class. When Paloma comes to the board and explains how she knows that the answer to the question, "How many $\frac{1}{4}$s are in 2?" is 8, she confidently and efficiently uses the Cuisenaire rods to justify her solution and provide her classmates with access to her thinking.
7e How Many $\frac{1}{3}$s Are in 2? Grade 6/Mr. Trenado	131	After Mr. Trenado introduces the problem, we see Yennifer and Ivelisse discussing the problem. How does Ivelisse use her understanding of how many thirds are in one to determine how many $\frac{1}{3}$s are in 2?	Much like Paloma in the previous clip (Video Clip 7d) Ivelisse first uses the Cuisenaire rods to show Yennifer that there are three $\frac{1}{3}$s in 1. Ivelisse then points to the second unit interval on the number line (the distance from 1 to 2) and explains that she needs another three ($\frac{1}{3}$s) because, as she says while pointing, "This is also one whole." She then mentally adds the $\frac{3}{3}$ from the first whole to the three $\frac{1}{3}$s from the second whole, to arrive at her answer of 6.
8a Multiplication Patterns Grade 4/Ms. Lee	143	In this clip, we see students building on their previous work with whole number multiplication to estimate the answer to multiplication problems involving fractions. Why is this a good task for beginning students' work with fraction multiplication?	Based on their previous experience, students often think that multiplication always "makes things bigger." By encouraging students to observe the patterns illustrated by the series of problems, Ms. Lee helps them consider what happens to products when the number that 6 is being multiplied by decreases from 8, to 4, to 2, to 1, to $\frac{1}{2}$. In this way, Ms. Lee prepares her students for reasoning about and discussing problems involving a whole number multiplied by a fraction.
8b Muhammad's Strategy for Adding $\frac{5}{9}$ and $\frac{8}{9}$ Grade 5/Ms. Kretschmar	144	In this clip, Lupe asks for help adding $\frac{5}{9}$ and $\frac{8}{9}$. We see Muhammad explaining his strategy for solving the problem. How does the written record of his work support Muhammad's explanation and help Lupe understand his strategy?	Students often have difficulty articulating the reasoning behind their approach to solving problems. By asking Muhammad to write down his strategy for decomposing $\frac{5}{9}$ in order to add it to $\frac{8}{9}$, Ms. Kretschmar validates Muhammad's method and also helps him become more aware of why his strategy makes sense. Muhammad's written record of his thinking also allows Lupe to understand how decomposing $\frac{5}{9}$ into $\frac{4}{9} + \frac{1}{9}$ made it easy to add to $\frac{8}{9}$ and get to the whole.

(continued)

Video Clip Number/ Title/Grade/Teacher	Page Number	Introduction	Observations
8c Using the Cuisenaire Rods to Explain Equivalent Fractions Grade 6/Mr. Trenado	145	In this clip, we see how Carlos uses the Cuisenaire rods to explain to his partner his reasoning about different ways to partition 1 minute (60 seconds). What ways does he share? How do the Cuisenaire rods support Carlos as he moves back and forth fluidly between the units of time—in other words, 1 minute and 60 seconds, and the fractional equivalents?	The Cuisenaire rods provide Carlos with a concrete referent for considering all the ways that the whole (in this case, 1 minute) can be partitioned—in halves, fourths, sixths, and thirds. Carlos is able to see and explain to his partner how the different rods represent different fractions of 1 minute. For example, the materials help the boys see how the light green rods represent $\frac{1}{4}$ of a minute because four of them are the same length as the rod representing the whole (minute). The rods help Carlos to simultaneously consider the whole as 1 minute and 60 seconds, so he is able to articulate how the light green rods also represent 15 seconds.
8d What Do You Notice About the Numerators and Denominators of Fractions Equal to $\frac{1}{2}$? Grade 5/Ms. Kretschmar and Ms. McNamara	146	Providing explicit opportunities for students to develop an understanding of benchmark fractions is an essential aspect of fraction instruction. This clip comes from a lesson in *Beyond Pizzas & Pies: 10 Essential Strategies for Supporting Fraction Sense, Second Edition* (McNamara and Shaughnessy 2015), in which students use Cuisenaire rods to partition number lines; chart fractions that are equal to, less than, and greater than $\frac{1}{2}$; and focus on the relationships between numerators and denominators. How can focusing on the relationship between numerators and denominators help students use $\frac{1}{2}$ as a benchmark fraction?	In order for students to understand fractional values, it is essential that they consider the relationship between the numerator and denominator and not focus on only the numerator or the denominator. For example, all fractions in which the numerator is equal to the denominator are equal to 1; all fractions in which numerator is half the denominator are equal to $\frac{1}{2}$; all fractions in which the numerator is one less than the denominator are one unit fraction away from 1; all fractions in which the numerator is greater than the denominator are greater than 1, etc. By focusing students on this relationship in fractions equal to $\frac{1}{2}$, teachers can help students understand $\frac{1}{2}$ as a benchmark fraction, and use this understanding as they encounter and talk about tasks involving fraction comparison and computation.

Video Clip Number/ Title/Grade/Teacher	Page Number	Introduction	Observations
8e Ms. Lee Revoices Ashley's Justification Grade 4/Ms. Lee	147	This clip takes place in the middle of a discussion of multiplication patterns. Students have solved the problems 6×8, 6×4, 6×2, and 6×1, and are discussing what 6 should be multiplied by next. After Ashley agrees that the next problem should be $6 \times \frac{1}{2}$, we hear the teacher revoicing her justification, based on the pattern of the previous problems. What purposes might Ms. Lee have had in revoicing Ashley's explanation?	Ms. Lee uses the talk move of revoicing Ashley's explanation to make sure that the other students can follow Ashley's thinking. Ashley is quite clear about how she knows that $\frac{1}{2}$ is the number that will follow the pattern in the series of problems, but Ms. Lee is also concerned with making sure other students can benefit from Ashley's thinking. Ms. Lee also reminds students of the idea of doubling, which was discussed previously, to help them consider the inverse relationship between doubling and halving.
8f Julian Restates Carlos's Answer Grade 6/Mr. Trenado	148	In this clip, which comes from Activity 7.2 in Chapter 7 (also labeled as Video Clip 7c), Carlos answers the question, "How many one-fourths are in one?" We then hear Mr Trenado ask a student to restate Carlos's answer. What benefits might come from asking students to restate each others' ideas?	There are several benefits to having students restate their classmates' ideas. When students restate, we can determine if the student who is restating truly understands the idea that was shared; we provide other students with an additional opportunity to consider and make sense of the idea being shared; we help students understand that they are responsible for listening to the explanations of their classmate; and we can encourage students to participate in classroom discussions even if they are not yet ready to share their own ideas.

(continued)

Video Clip Number/ Title/Grade/Teacher	Page Number	Introduction	Observations
8g Multiple Students Share Their Reasoning About Placing $\frac{1}{2}$ on the Number Line Grade 5/Ms. Kretschmar	149	In this clip, which comes from Activity 1.3 in Chapter 1 (also labeled as Video Clip 1a), we watch as four students share their reasoning about where to place $\frac{1}{2}$ on a 0–4 number line. How do these ideas help shape the conversation and provide the teacher with important information about what students do and don't understand?	By asking students to respond to each other's ideas, Ms. Kretschmar is provided with a great deal of information about how her students are approaching this task. Had she stepped in after hearing only from Lupe, she would have missed the opportunity to hear from Juan and find out how he was thinking about where to place $\frac{1}{2}$ on the number line. As students continue to share their thinking it becomes obvious that there is quite a bit of confusion in the class. As Ms. Kretschmar highlights the three ideas being presented and asks students to discuss them, she is using students' answers, both correct and incorrect, as valid mathematical ideas that are worthy of consideration, discussion, and refinement.
8h "Tell Us More About That" Grade 4/Ms. McNamara	150	In this clip, Astrid tells the class that she knows that the answer to $6 \times 2\frac{1}{2}$ is between 12 and 20. The teacher prompts her to add on to her response by saying, "Tell us more about that." Astrid goes on to share how she came up with her answer. How does Ms. McNamara's prompt help the students understand what a complete answer involves?	In classrooms focusing on mathematical discourse, it is often necessary to teach students what is involved in providing a complete answer because students may be used to answering questions in math class with a one-word response. This kind of response provides little information for the teacher or other students regarding how the answer was achieved or why it makes sense. By asking the student to "tell us more about that," Ms. McNamara is helping students understand that complete answers include not only a response to the question, but also a rationale for the response.

Video Clip Number/Title/Grade/Teacher	Page Number	Introduction	Observations
8i Posing a "Thinking Question" Grade 4/Ms. McNamara	151	In this clip, we see the introduction to a lesson in *Beyond Pizzas & Pies: 10 Essential Strategies for Supporting Fraction Sense, Second Edition* (McNamara and Shaughnessy 2015), in which students find the fractional relationships between different pattern blocks. To establish the idea that part–whole relationships depend on knowing both the part and the whole, students are asked to provide the fraction name for the triangle. The teacher provides several seconds for students to come up with an answer, telling them that this is a "thinking question." After several students have provided ideas, the teacher continues by establishing the idea that to know the fraction name for the triangle, you must also know which pattern block is being used as the whole. What is the purpose of wait time and how does it help students in this clip?	Of all the talk moves that teachers use, wait time is the simplest in theory but often the most difficult to execute in practice. By telling students that the question being posed is a "thinking question," Ms. McNamara lets students know that they are all expected to think about the question and come up with an answer. This is in contrast to many classrooms in which the majority of students sit passively because they know the questions posed by the teacher will be answered by the student who shouts out the answer or whose hand goes up first. By waiting more than ten seconds before calling on anyone, Ms. McNamara gives all students time to consider the question and formulate their answer, which is especially important for students whose first language is not English.

Video Clip Number/ Title/Grade/Teacher	Page Number	Introduction	Observations
6d, 6f, 7d, and 7e Teachers' Use of Turn and Talk	152	Revisit these clips. Each clip shows teachers using turn and talk as a strategy for preparing students to share their thinking during whole-class discussion. You will see how several of the strategies included in this chapter are just as beneficial to students when they talk in small groups as they are when they are engaged in discussion with the whole class. What impact might the use of turn and talk have on students' contributions to whole-group discussions?	Using turn and talk allows all students to engage in mathematical discourse in a much less formal context than that of whole-class discussion. As we watch the clips we see students try out their ideas, consider the ideas of others, practice explaining and justifying their thinking to their partners, and refine their use of academic language. In addition, when students are engaged in turn and talk the teacher can quickly gauge where students are in their understanding. This is especially evident in Video Clip 6d when, in response to Ms. Lee's question, "What factor goes in this blank?" we hear several students call out "Zero!" Finally, the use of turn and talk sends a clear message to students that they are all mathematical thinkers with ideas that contribute to the development of the collective understandings of the classroom community.

References

How to Use This Resource

Carpenter, T. P. 2014. "Building on Intuitive Understanding." The Doing What Works Library. Available at: http://wested.mediacore.tv/media/building-on-intuitive-understanding

McNamara, Julie, and Meghan M. Shaughnessy. 2015. *Beyond Pizzas & Pies: 10 Essential Strategies for Supporting Fraction Sense, Grades 3–5.* 2d ed. Sausalito, CA: Math Solutions.

Chapter 1

Armstrong, Barbara E., and Carol N. Larson. 1995. Students' Use of Part–Whole Direct Comparison Strategies for Comparing Partitioned Rectangles. *Journal for Research in Mathematics Education* 26: 2–19.

Davydov, V. V., and Z. H. Tsetkovich. 1992. On the Objective Origin of the Concept of Fractions. *Focus on Learning Problems in Mathematics* 13: 13–61.

Lamon, Susan L. 2007. Rational Numbers and Proportional Reasoning: Toward a Theoretical Framework for Research. In *Second Handbook of Research on Mathematics Teaching and Learning,* ed. Fred Lester, 629–67. Reston, VA: NCTM.

Mack, Nancy K. 1995. Confounding Whole Number and Fraction Concepts When Building on Informal Knowledge. *Journal for Research in Mathematics Education* 26: 422–41.

———. 1990. Learning Fractions with Understanding: Building on Informal Knowledge. *Journal for Research in Mathematics Education* 21: 16–32.

McNamara, Julie, and Meghan M. Shaughnessy. 2015. *Beyond Pizzas & Pies: 10 Essential Strategies for Supporting Fraction Sense, Grades 3–5.* 2d ed. Sausalito, CA: Math Solutions.

National Governors Association Center for Best Practices and the Council of State School Officers. 2010. *Common Core State Standards Initiative: Common Core State Standards for Mathematics,* www.corestandards.org/Math

National Research Council. 2001. *Adding It Up: Helping Children Learn Mathematics,* eds. J. Kilpatrick, J. Swafford, and B. Findell. Washington, DC: National Academy Press.

Richardson, Kathy. 2008. "The Algorithm: Have Our Students Really Learned What They Need to Know?" Presented at the annual conference of the National Council of Teachers of Mathematics, April 2008, Salt Lake City, Utah.

Siegler, Robert, Thomas Carpenter, Francis (Skip) Fennell, David Geary, James Lewis, Yukari Okamoto, Laurie Thompson, and Jonathan Wray. 2010. *Developing Effective Fractions Instruction for Kindergarten Through 8th Grade: A Practice Guide*. NCEE#2010-4039. Washington, DC: National Center for Education Evaluation and Regional Assistance, Institute of Education Sciences, U.S. Department of Education.

Wu, Hung-Hsi. 2014. Teaching Fractions According to the Common Core Standards. http://math.berkeley.edu/~wu/CCSS-Fractions_1.pdf.

———. 2002. Chapter 2: Fractions (Draft). http://math.berkeley.edu/~wu/EMI2a.pdf.

———. 1999. Some Remarks on the Teaching of Fractions in Elementary School. http://math.berkeley.edu/~wu/fractions2.pdf.

Chapter 2

Carpenter, Thomas P., Elizabeth Fennema, Megan L. Franke, Linda Levi, and Susan B. Empson. 1999. *Children's Mathematics: Cognitively Guided Instruction*. Portsmouth, NH: Heinemann.

Cramer, Kathleen, Terry Wyberg, and Seth Leavitt. 2008. The Role of Representations in Fraction Addition and Subtraction. *Mathematics Teaching in the Middle School* 13: 490–96.

Dixon, Juli K., and Jennifer M. Tobias. 2013. The Whole Story: Understanding Fraction Computation. *Mathematics Teaching in the Middle School* 19: 156–63.

National Governors Association Center for Best Practices and the Council of State School Officers. 2010. *Common Core State Standards Initiative: Common Core State Standards for Mathematics*, www.corestandards.org/Math

Verschaffel, Lieven, Brian Greer, and Eric de Corte. 2000. Making Sense of Word Problems. *Educational Studies in Mathematics* 42: 211–13.

Chapter 3

Ashlock, Robert B. 2010. *Error Patterns in Computation: Using Error Patterns to Help Each Student Learn*. 10th ed. Boston: Allyn & Bacon.

Bresser, Rusty, and Caron Holzman. 2006. *Developing Number Sense, Grades 3–6*. Sausalito, CA: Math Solutions.

Burns, Marilyn. 2003. *Lessons for Extending Fractions, Grade 5.* Sausalito, CA: Math Solutions.

Carpenter, Thomas P., Elizabeth Fennema, Megan L. Franke, Linda Levi, and Susan B. Empson. 1999. *Children's Mathematics: Cognitively Guided Instruction.* Portsmouth, NH: Heinemann.

Department of Education. Institute of Education Sciences. National Center for Education Statistics. (11/05/2002–), "National Assessment of Educational Progress (NAEP) Data Files", http://hdl.handle.net/1902.5/609759 National Archives and Records Administration [Distributor] V1 [Version].

National Governors Association Center for Best Practices and the Council of State School Officers. 2010. *Common Core State Standards Initiative: Common Core State Standards for Mathematics,* www.corestandards.org/Math.

Petit, Marjorie M., Robert E. Laird, and Edwin L. Marsden. 2010. *A Focus on Fractions: Bringing Researching to the Classroom.* New York: Routledge.

Chapter 4

Bresser, Rusty, and Caron Holzman. 2006. *Developing Number Sense, Grades 3–6.* Sausalito, CA: Math Solutions.

Dixon, Juli K., and Jennifer M. Tobias. 2013. The Whole Story: Understanding Fraction Computation. *Mathematics Teaching in the Middle School* 19: 156–63.

Van Den Heuvel-Panhuizen, Maria. 2003. The Didactical Use of Models in Realistic Mathematics Education: An Example from a Longitudinal Trajectory on Percentage. *Educational Studies in Mathematics* 54: 9–35.

Chapter 5

Carpenter, Thomas P., Elizabeth Fennema, Megan L. Franke, Linda Levi, and Susan B. Empson. 1999. *Children's Mathematics: Cognitively Guided Instruction.* Portsmouth, NH: Heinemann.

Fosnot, C.T., and M. Dolk, 2002. *Young Mathematicians at Work: Constructing Fractions, Decimals, and Percents.* Portsmouth, NH: Heinemann.

National Governors Association Center for Best Practices and the Council of State School Officers. 2010. *Common Core State Standards Initiative: Common Core State Standards for Mathematics,* www.corestandards.org/Math

Wyberg, Terry, Stephanie W. Whitney, Kathleen A. Cramer, Debra S. Monson, and Seth Leavitt. 2012. Unfolding Fraction Multiplication. *Mathematics Teaching in the Middle School* 17: 289–94.

Chapter 6

Bresser, Rusty, and Caron Holzman. 2006. *Developing Number Sense, Grades 3–6*. Sausalito, CA: Math Solutions.

Burns, Marilyn. 2003. *Lessons for Extending Fractions, Grade 5*. Sausalito, CA: Math Solutions.

Seeley, Cathy L. 2009. *Faster Isn't Smarter: Messages About Math, Teaching, and Learning in the 21st Century: a Resource for Teachers, Leaders, Policy Makers, and Families*. Sausalito, CA: Math Solutions.

Chapter 7

Newton, Kristie J., and Janice Sands. 2012. Why Don't We Just Divide Across? *Mathematics Teaching in the Middle School* 17: 341–45.

Tirosh, Dina. 2000. Enhancing Prospective Teachers' Knowledge of Children's Conceptions: The Case of Division of Fractions. *Journal for Research in Mathematics Education* 31: 5–25.

Chapter 8

Chapin, Suzanne H., Catherine O'Connor, and Nancy C. Anderson. 2013. *Classroom Discussions in Math: A Teacher's Guide for Using Talk Moves to Support the Common Core and More, Grades K–6*. 3d ed. Sausalito, CA: Math Solutions.

McNamara, Julie, and Meghan M. Shaughnessy. 2015. *Beyond Pizzas & Pies: 10 Essential Strategies for Supporting Fraction Sense, Grades 3–5*. 2d ed. Sausalito, CA: Math Solutions.

National Governors Association Center for Best Practices and the Council of State School Officers. 2010. *Common Core State Standards Initiative: Common Core State Standards for Mathematics,* www.corestandards.org/Math

Math Solutions Publications is now part of Heinemann.
To learn more about our resources and authors please visit
www.Heinemann.com/Math.

Index